FROM PUBLIC STREETS TO PRIVATE LIVES

For my parents, Brenda and Jack.

From Public Streets
to Private Lives

The changing task of social work

VIVIENE E. CREE
Department of Social Work
University of Edinburgh

Avebury

Aldershot · Brookfield USA · Hong Kong · Singapore · Sydney

© Viviene E. Cree 1995

Published by
Avebury
Ashgate Publishing Limited
Gower House
Croft Road
Aldershot
Hants GU11 3HR
England

Ashgate Publishing Company
Old Post Road
Brookfield
Vermont 05036
USA

British Library Cataloguing in Publication Data

Cree, Viviene E.
    From Public Streets to Private Lives: Changing
    Task of Social Work
    I. Title
    361.3
 ISBN 1-85628-847-1

Library of Congress Cataloging-in-Publication Data

Cree, Viviene E., 1954–
From public streets to private lives: the changing task of
social work / Viviene E. Cree
        p.   cm.
    Includes bibliographical references.
    ISBN 1-85628-847-1: $51.95
    1. Family Care (Agency) – History. 2. Family services –
Scotland – History. 3. Social service – Scotland – History.
I. Title.
HV700.S32C74 1995   94-35597
362.82.82'8'09411–dc20   CIP

Printed and bound by Athenæum Press Ltd.,
Gateshead, Tyne & Wear.

Contents

Figures

Acknowledgements

I am indebted to Family Care's staff and committee members (past and present) for making this book possible - for giving me their time and their knowledge, and for allowing me access to records, documents and archives. My thanks go also to all those who played a part as external respondents, and gave me a broader picture of social work in Scotland. It is important to state that whilst wishing to give credit to the respondents for their insights and their experience, all interpretation of events is mine alone.

I would like to thank all the staff at Edinburgh University who have given me advice and encouragement throughout the process of my Ph.D. and beyond. Special thanks go to my Ph.D. supervisors, Ralph Davidson and Beverley Brown, and to my Ph.D. examiners, Lynn Jamieson (Edinburgh University) and Margaret Yelloly (Tavistock Clinic). Thanks also to Lindsay Paterson and Veronica O'Malley for advice on technical presentation.

Most of all, I wish to thank my parents, my family and friends, especially Colin, Calum and Iain, who have lived through this research and writing project with me, and have supported me throughout.

Introduction

My aim in writing this book is to contribute to a better understanding of social work - to help to make sense of the confusing, multi-layered, contradictory nature of social work policy and practice today. I will argue that social work is best understood as a discursive formation, that is, a collection of competing and contradictory discourses that come together at a particular moment in time to frame the task of social work, defining not just its capabilities, but also its potential. I will argue that there is no essential social work task. Rather, social work has always been subject to competing claims of definition and practice. It is therefore only by exploring some of the discourses within social work that we can begin to understand what social work is and what it might be.

I have chosen to study the discursive formation of social work by looking inward and looking back, using the case study of the development of one influential Scottish voluntary social work agency (Family Care) as a vehicle for exploring the changing nature of the social work task. Family Care, although in many ways a unique and specialised agency, offers in its historical development over the last eighty years access to some of the key debates and concerns which have been central to the formation of the social work task. In Family Care's story we can see different discourses within social work struggling for prominence.

There are two fundamental beliefs underpinning my work. The first is that we cannot understand the present without considering the past - the present is in fact made up of threads and ideas from the past. (Foucault, 1972). I believe that to begin to understand social work today we must look at its historical development, at the ideas and practices which have survived as well as those which have been jettisoned along the way. Social work is full

1

of continuities and discontinuities, repetitions and reversals. All have something to tell us about social work, and give us clues as to how social work may be developing in the future.

My second belief is in the intrinsic value of the case study. Case studies allow us to look inside organisations - to see specific and unusual events as well as general themes which occur across different settings. (Mitchell, 1983.) It is in the special examples provided by an in-depth study of one agency that we come across surprising material, and uncover new knowledge about what might seem to be a familiar subject. This does not, of course, imply that I can tell the whole story of the history of social work by examining one Scottish voluntary agency (albeit an agency which grew out of a national organisation). What I can describe is the development of one key strand of social work, as it negotiates with, and intersects with other kinds of social work in other settings. The history of Family Care provides an opportunity to look at how and why changes have taken place in social work, as well as illuminating the actual detail of the changes themselves.

It is important to be clear from the beginning that this is not an evaluative study aimed as assessing social work effectiveness. I am not concerned with how successful the product of social work has been, or with levels of satisfaction with social work intervention. Instead my focus is on the *meaning* of social work, encapsulated in the term the social work task - that is, the complex inter-relationship between what social workers do, why they do it, and what society thinks they ought to do. (Barclay, 1982.)

Material for the book is drawn from research carried out for a Ph.D., completed in November 1992. In carrying out the research, I had access to agency records (annual reports, committee minutes and case notes) which were almost complete for eighty years. I also interviewed eighty six respondents - managers, committee members and social workers, going as far back as the 1920s. By pulling together a synthesis of documentary evidence, material from interviews, and wide background reading on social work and social welfare history, I have been able to paint a highly individual and yet well grounded picture of changes within the world of social work since the beginning of the twentieth century. (See Appendix for a full description of Research Methods .)

This book is very much an "insider's" account. I have worked in social work practice and teaching for eighteen years, seven of which were spent working as a social worker and social work practice teacher at Family Care. The research is rooted in the doubts, questions and ambivalence which I have about social work - about its relationship with the state, about its social control function, and about its central role in relation to women and families.

I see my involvement as a strength in the study, and believe that "passionate scholarship" (Du Bois, 1983) which is reflexive and prepared to admit its value and knowledge base is of much greater value than research which pretends to be neutral and "scientific". My personal and professional engagement with social work and with this agency in particular has brought a depth of insight into my subject which would otherwise never have been possible. I have been my first respondent as well as a self-critical researcher. (Stanley and Wise, 1983.)

Family Care - a brief history

Family Care began its life in 1911 as a branch of an international organisation known as the National Vigilance Association (NVA). The agency's work (in common with all National Vigilance Association branches throughout the world) centred on prostitution, sexual behaviour and the "white slave trade" - rescuing young women who were deemed to be at risk of sexual exploitation at home and abroad, and pressing for legislation to control sexual conduct.

By the 1940s, the agency had shifted its focus away from vigilance concerns towards a casework service, and in 1947 the agency (now known as the Guild of Service) opened the first family group home in Scotland. The agency held a position of dominance in developing professional approaches to child care and social work from the 1940s to the 1970s. It pioneered the development of a professional approach to adoption assessment, and led the field in placing children previously considered "unadoptable" for adoption; and in preparing children for new families. The agency played a key role as the Scottish representative on the influential Adoption Resource Exchange in London, and later developed a more local matching service for "hard to place" children. The Guild of Service's reputation for good practice was such that successive generations of Scottish social work students spent part of their training in the agency.

Since the 1980s, the agency's fortunes have been mixed. Family Care (another name-change in 1978) illustrates well the difficulties faced by medium sized, specialist voluntary agencies confronted by the vast power of statutory Social Work Departments. At the present time, the agency is in crisis, fighting a rear-guard action to hold onto some of the services which it has developed over recent years - an adoption counselling service, a community based project for women and children, and a volunteer befriending scheme.

3

Structure of the book

This book is structured around six main discourses which have come together and assumed significance at different points in Family Care's history - vigilance discourse; Christian ethics; professionalism; psy discourses; discourses addressing women; and welfare discourses. I will examine each discourse in a broadly chronological way, recognising that this does not, of course, imply that one strand begins when another ends. On the contrary, there is a large measure of overlap between the areas under discussion. This overlap, and the relation between different discourses, forms the core of my analysis of the changing task of social work.

Chapter One sets the scene for the book, locating the theoretical approach which I have adopted firmly in the context of feminist and Foucauldian analysis. Here I will argue that Foucauldian ideas of discourse and power are useful in explaining and enriching our understandings of the contradictory nature of the social work task.

Chapter Two describes the beginnings of the agency in the National Vigilance Association (NVA), an agency which was not itself a social work agency, but which grew out of the nineteenth century social purity movement. I will examine the eclipse of the vigilance movement, and suggest that although moral discourses have been overtaken by new professional, legal and psycho-analytic discourses, they have not disappeared completely. I will look at vigilance discourse today, asking what role social work currently plays in moral policing.

Chapter Three argues that moral and Christian discourses which have been central to social work's value base and practices, remain of fundamental importance today, though couched in different language. I suggest that the standard account of the secularisation of social work is unconvincing - that churches of all denominations continue to be heavily involved in social work, and that many individual social workers (as evidenced by this research), continue to see their work as a vocation and a kind of service.

Chapter Four explores the related issues of professions and professionalisation, and asks why social work wished to professionalise itself. I will describe professionalisation as it has affected this agency, and the gains and the losses (intended and unintended) to the agency and its personnel. The story of the professionalisation of social work has been a popular one. We are all familiar with tales of "ladies bountiful", of "do-gooders" and of their displacement in the era of professionalisation. My account challenges this stereotype, and presents a more complex picture.

Chapter Five examines the notion that something resembling a "psychiatric deluge" may have taken place in British social work. Family Care was in the forefront of new ideas and practices, and is well placed to examine the impact of psychological and psycho-analytic ideas on social work. Arising out of this, I will explore the evolution of social work's focus on the needs of children.

Chapter Six gives prominence to the competing and contradictory discourses around women in this agency and in social work - women in their positions as service users, service providers and service managers. This book is unapologetically a women's story. Family Care is an organisation which has always been a women's organisation, with women clients, women workers, and women managers. It therefore provides an ideal opportunity to examine the seeming paradox that a woman's occupation such as social work has been responsible for promulgating a specific set of sexist assumptions about women and their role in the family and in society.

Chapter Seven turns to the relationship between statutory and voluntary welfare discourses. I will explore the way in which the balance has shifted over who should and can provide social welfare, and consider the place of a voluntary agency such as this one, in the new world of community care and the market economy.

Chapter Eight presents a summary of the main themes in the book, and looks forward to examine the future task for social work in the years ahead. I will conclude that because social work's history is characterised by continuity and change, current debates over the role of the state in welfare provision can best be understood by a historical analysis.

Research Methods are discussed in an Appendix at the end of the book.

1 Conceptual framework

The conceptual starting point for this book lies in two different and initially unconnected threads - feminism and Foucault. As a feminist sociologist working in social work, I set out to carry out a piece of research which would advance knowledge and understanding of the place of women in social work - as primary service providers and service users. At the same time I was determined to give space to some of the unheard women's voices in the history of social work - the ordinary social workers (paid and unpaid) who had devoted their lives to improving social services and building their profession. Feminist research offered a way of proceeding which allowed for a "conscious subjectivity" (Duelli-Klein, 1983) - an involvement in the research process, and a way of seeing the connections between individual experience and wider structural issues, that is, the personal as political.

Foucault's analysis of history, discourse and power provided the conceptual means for achieving my feminist objectives. This is not to suggest that the book is a strict attempt at an application of Foucault's method, or a detailed examination of his ideas. Instead, a Foucauldian perspective has enabled me to deal with the ambiguities, contradictions and complexities which are an integral part of social work discourse. I have learned that instead of looking for ways of resolving these contradictions, the contradictions are themselves the key towards understanding the nature of the social work task.

At the time I began my research, there was little published material to help me to explore fundamental disagreements between feminism and Foucault, particularly around Foucault's conception of power and resistance. Since then, however, new feminist scholarship has begun to examine the possibilities of developing a Foucauldian feminism. I will discuss this work in relation to my own theoretical position, after I have described the key ideas which I have drawn from Foucault's writing.

Foucault - discourse, power and knowledge

Foucault presents a very particular way of thinking about the social world in which we live. He rejects "grand" theories which set out to explain all human behaviour in a single unity, and introduces instead a theoretical position based on complexity, contradiction and duality. He is not interested in "ideologies" viewed as one sided truths which are imposed on individuals, or are somehow held in common. He proposes instead an analysis based on the creative capabilities of discourse, knowledge and power. For Foucault, discourse is much more than simply verbal representation or even a way of thinking and producing meaning. Discourses are "practices that systematically form the objects of which they speak." (Foucault, 1972, p.49.)

Foucault argues that it is through discourses, that is, the mix of beliefs, ideas and concepts which make up and organise our relation to reality, that power and knowledge come together. Discourses are ways of constituting knowledge - of regulating what is and is not held to be true by a given society at a particular historical moment in time. Foucault continues:-

> ...truth isn't outside power or lacking in power... Each society has its own regime of truth, its "general politics" of truth: that is, the types of discourse which it accepts and makes function as true; the mechanisms and instances which enable one to distinguish true and false statements... (Gordon, 1980, p. 131.)

Knowledge is therefore not singular or uncomplicated, the sum of what is thought to be true. It is "the whole set of practices, singularities and deviations of which one could speak in a discourse." (Foucault, 1972, p. 182.) In other words, specific forms of knowledge are created through power. Again, power is not presented as a negative concept which exists only to forbid and repress. For Foucault, it is omnipresent, diffused throughout society, both regulatory and productive:-

> Power is everywhere; not because it embraces everything, but because it comes from everywhere... Power is not an institution, and not a structure; neither is it a certain strength we are endowed with; it is the name that one attributes to a complex strategical situation in a particular society. (Foucault, 1976, pp. 92-93.)

And where there is power, there is resistance - "points of resistance are present everywhere in the power network." (Foucault, 1976, p. 95.) Not

7

only resistance, but a "plurality of resistances" which are an essential part of the exercise of power.

Foucault has been criticised for presenting too abstract a concept of power and resistance. It is claimed that in his desire to distance himself from a Marxist analysis of the state he lost sight of the real inequalities in power relations in society. Mort (1987) argues that resistance is rarely a spontaneous eruption from below. Instead, resistance needs a specific language to articulate demands and endow protests with meaning. (Mort, 1987, p. 218.)

In his later writing and interviews, Foucault explains that his early analysis of power must be understood in the context of the 1960's, a time when power was being defined in terms of prohibition. He asserts:- "It seemed to me that power was something much more complex than that." (Foucault, 1978, in Kritzman, 1988, p. 102.) He argues that what he had set out to do in his studies of madness, of sexuality, and of punishment, was to examine the strategies and mechanisms of power - "all those techniques by which a decision is accepted and by which that decision could not but be taken in the way it was." (Op. cit., p. 104.) Foucault revised his position on power, making a distinction between domination, where the subject is unable to overturn the dominant relation, and power, where resistance is always possible. (See Foucault, 1984, in Bernauer and Rasmussen, 1988, pp. 12-13.)

Viewed from a Foucauldian perspective, social work knowledge (social work "truth") is not a singular phenomenon, forced on us from on high, by some all powerful patriarchal state ideological apparatus. Instead, it is constituted by all the discourses contained within it; discourses which struggle to name, classify and regulate it. All of those involved in social work (managers, social workers, service users, politicians, the press and the general public) have a part to play in creating the discursive formation which is social work - in building the knowledge, values and beliefs which are central to social work, and in putting into place the strategies and the day to day practices which are established arising out of those interpretations and meanings. In writing a history of social work, I will be writing a history of what certain discourses have had to say about social work - about its purpose and its goals, its subjects and its objects, its parameters and its aspirations, that is, its *task*.

My job as a researcher becomes not to try to uncover the hidden "truths" about social work, but instead to seek out "the ensemble of rules according to which the true and the false are separated and specific effects of power attached to the true." (Gordon, 1980, p. 132.) It is to the various discourses that we must turn to begin to understand social work, witnessed in the minute details of social practices as well as the written documents and the things which respondents say, and do not say.

Foucault and history

In "The Archaeology of Knowledge" (1972), Foucault outlines for the first time his historical methodology, and presents a systematic attack on the history of ideas. He rejects traditional evolutionary, linear approaches to history which present change in terms of continuity and transition, and which assume that there is a natural unfolding towards an end which has been implicitly there in its origins. He writes:-

> We must rid ourselves of a whole mass of notions, each of which, in its own way, diversifies from the theme of continuity ... Once these immediate forms of continuity are suspended, an entire field is set free. (Foucault, 1972, pp. 21 and 26.)

Foucault argues that change and transformation must be understood in terms of discontinuity as well as continuity. He points to what are often small scale changes in every day living which signify larger reversals in discursive practices - moments when there is a rearrangement in the various layers of power and knowledge. And he argues that not all dimensions of society change at the same time, or in a uniform way. He warns that when we come across something new, there is no absolute origin, and no total revolution. (Foucault, 1972, pp. 173-175.)

As well as criticising evolutionary models of history, Foucault challenges the notion that there is coherence in discourse. He suggest that conventionally, faced with an irregularity, historians will seek to explain this by uncovering some hidden coherence. He urges instead that "contradictions are neither appearances to be overcome, nor secret principles to be uncovered. They are objects to be described in themselves." (Foucault, 1972, p. 151.) He continues:-

> A discursive formation is not therefore an ideal, continuous smooth text that runs beneath the multiplicity of contradictions, and resolves them in the calm unity of coherent thought... It is rather a space of multiple dissensions; a set of different oppositions whose levels and roles must be described. (Foucault, 1972, p. 155.)

This perspective has been central to my analysis, as I have sought to identify moments when shifts have taken place, and to understand the meaning of those shifts. The history of social work reflects a number of interweaving and at times contradictory themes. There are moments when history seems to repeat itself - when "new" ideas emerge which have been forgotten from before. There are also occasions when there is dispute between different participants within social work. The development of social work has been characterised by swings for and against particular solutions to identified problems. A Foucauldian approach offers a way of making sense of this by concentrating on the actual practices (discourses) which signify these developments and discontinuities.

Foucault's critique of the evolutionary approach is also useful. Linear views of history assume that things are getting better, or getting worse - that social progress is taking place, through greater reason, rationality and technological development, or that we are all headed for eventual disaster. My research into social work's history leads me to a different set of conclusions. The history of social work is not the story of ever increasing knowledge, expertise and human enlightenment. Neither is it the story of an ever expanding state machine designed to find ever sophisticated ways of controlling the working class or women. On the contrary, every new intervention in social work has been accompanied by both gains and losses along the way, and consequences which are not always expected or predictable. We need to find ways of understanding the story of social work which are reflexive and which forefront the conflicts and contradictions inherent in the social work task.

In order to find a practical way of keeping Foucault's insights at the core of my research I have drawn on six broad questions adapted from Foucault's methodology. These are as follows:-

1   When did new ideas and practices (discontinuities) emerge? Why should they have emerged now?

2   Who is speaking, and what is said and not said? (that is, who has the power/ authority to define the social work task?)

3   Where does the discourse come from? What are the institutional sites from where it derives its legitimate source and point of application? (for example, university, professional associations, government?)

4   What positions can the subjects (social workers) of the discourse adopt, and how does this relate to the changing positions of other groups? (for example, clergy, doctors, clients?)

5   How are the objects (client groups or social problems) formed, and once formed, divided, classified and related to and from one another?

6   What are the concepts, that is, the perceived solutions/ strategies which

are presented to resolve perceived problems?

A Foucauldian feminism?

Recent feminist writing has sought either to bring Foucault and feminism together into a Foucauldian feminism (Sawicki, 1991), or to explore the tensions between Foucault and feminism (Cooper, 1994; Ramazanoglu, 1993; Smart, 1989 and 1992).

My perspective is more intuitive than intellectual. Foucault's ideas on power - its relationality and its productivity - make sense to me in trying to understand social work, and in particular women's relation to the task of social work. Social work is fraught with ambiguities and paradoxes which centre on women. Is social work's primary function to care for or to control women and children? If it is only about controlling women, why do they (women) put up with it, and why do so many women choose social work as a career? Is the family the source of women's oppression as some feminists suggest? And is community care policy a deliberate strategy to subjugate women? If so, how do we account for the fact that most people prefer to stay at home, and women on the whole want to care for their dependent relatives? And what about the very many feminists who are working in social work? Are they (we) misguided fools, or is a feminist social work ever possible?

The more I have learned about social work's history, the less convinced I am by "grand" theories which place their explanations in terms of capitalism or patriarchy. Unless we are willing to write off generations of women in terms of "false consciousness" (which clearly I am not prepared to do) then we must find a way of explaining women's complicity in the social work task. The "truth" as I see it is that women have historically had a lot to gain from social work - particularly as service providers and managers - and service users themselves have played a part in determining the kind of service which they receive.

Those of us who have worked in social work know that the reality of social workers' power and authority is that it is both limited and subscribed - limited because of resistance from clients, and subscribed by the state through legislation. At the same time, its power is awesome, as anyone faced with a social work investigation will testify. Social work power is not just about repressive power - about what people can and cannot do - it is also productive. It can encourage new, more positive ways of behaving, and help to safeguard rights of women and children, and vulnerable groups and individuals. A simple feminist analysis which identifies power in terms of patriarchy does not afford the depth of understanding needed for coming to

11

terms with the very contradictory relationship which we as women have with the task of social work. Social work has been and to a large extent remains a women's profession. Despite the almost total absence of women in senior management, especially in statutory agencies, social work is still today carried out on the whole by women for women - by women social workers, home helps and care assistants for women as mothers, daughters and partners. These realities are best explained by drawing on a Foucauldian feminist approach.

Finally, I find Foucault's perspective an optimistic one. If power is not total, and discourse is always the site of conflict and contestation, then change is possible. We as women in social work have a chance to influence and to challenge - to work to create a social work task which is both anti-oppressive and supportive to women and children.

2 Vigilance and the social purity movement

Introduction

The voluntary organisation known today as Family Care began in 1911 as a local branch of a national vigilance organisation formed in 1885 which had branches throughout Britain and connections throughout the world. The National Vigilance Association (NVA) of Scotland (Eastern Division) did not define itself as a social work agency. Its purpose, in common with other vigilance branches and associations, was to protect women and girls "against outrage, abduction and prostitution, and the terrible wickedness and cruelty of the White Slave Trade."[1] This protection was to be achieved through a range of activities - through legislation, anti-pornography campaigns, sex education, action against brothels, and a strong physical presence by the patrolling of streets, docks and railway stations, and by attendance at police and sheriff courts.

Three questions must be addressed here. First, how was it that an organisation like the NVA came into existence with such popular appeal at the end of the nineteenth and beginning of the twentieth centuries? Second, how did this organisation come to be transformed into a social work agency? Third, what has happened to the vigilance discourse today? What role is there for contemporary social work as guardian angel of private and public morality?

I believe that the vigilance story, which at first glance may seem like an episode from a different era, has important implications and consequences for us today. At the social policy level, it is in the rise of the vigilance movement that we see a consensus being reached for the first time about the state having a legitimate right to intervene in the private, sexual lives of individuals. Hand in hand with this, we see the emergence of the characterisation of women and children as being in need of special protection and surveillance. At the social work practice level, social workers today struggle with complex questions of rights and responsibilities, private and public concerns, centred on the familiar vigilance concern - women and children at sexual risk. Feminists inside and outside social work then and now find themselves on opposing sides of the social purity debate - both for and against prostitution and its control; both for and against the control of pornography; both for and against an increase in state control over individual behaviour.

Prostitution - the great social evil

The passing of the Criminal Law (Amendment) Act on 14 August 1885, and the formation one week later of the National Vigilance Association, set up to be the instrument which would monitor and support the new legislation, cannot be understood except as the final stage in a battle over prostitution which had been waged throughout the nineteenth century, at times reaching fever-pitch. James Miller writing in 1859 illustrates the strength of feeling on the subject of prostitution in Scotland:-

> Let anyone walk certain streets of London, Glasgow or Edinburgh of a night, and without troubling his head with statistics, his eyes and ears will tell him at once what a multitudinous amazonian army the devil keeps in constant field service, for advancing his own ends. The stones seem alive with lust, and the very atmosphere is tainted. (Miller, 1859, p. 5.)

Prostitution was more than just private sexual conduct. It was symbolic of social evil, the outward manifestation of the underlying problems of urban life. (Logan, 1871.) And while prostitution symbolised social evil, immorality was believed to be related to (and sometimes the cause of) poor housing, overcrowding, squalor, disease, and the threat of the working class. Even cholera epidemics and typhoid were blamed first and foremost on a lack of morality in working-class people. (Mort, 1987.)

Concern over prostitution was heightened during the mid nineteenth century with the campaign for and against the imposition of the Contagious Diseases (CD) Acts. The discovery of the impact of venereal disease on the physical condition of the armed forces was the lever which forced the prostitution debate out of the realm of religious and moral dispute right into the heart of the scientific and political domain.

14

Contagious Diseases Acts of 1864, 1866, and 1869

The government, intent on upgrading and professionalising the army, needed a way of controlling the spread of venereal disease, and modern "scientific" procedures to control prostitution were introduced as a means towards achieving this end. The CD Acts of 1864, 1866 and 1869 legislated for the registration, examination and isolation of women who were believed to be working as prostitutes.

The 1864 Act targeted eleven military stations, garrisons and seaport towns in southern England and in Ireland, where plain clothes police officers acting on information supplied by paid informers were given powers to arrest and take for registration and internal examination any woman thought to be working as a prostitute. Women found to have venereal disease could then be detained in a certified Lock Hospital for up to nine months. In 1866 and again in 1869, the Act was repealed and re-enacted, strengthening its powers and extending the geographical limits of its jurisdiction. (Bland and Mort, 1984; Prochaska, 1980.)

But the control of prostitution was far from being an unproblematic exercise. The CD Acts caused a huge controversy, with individuals and groups aligned for and against their institution. What was at stake here was not simply the behaviour of a few "immoral" women - the CD Acts were regarded as a matter of individual liberty versus state control, and a battle over the right to define and control behaviour. The CD Acts signified a contest over who had the authority/power to "speak" about prostitution and sexual behaviour; about where the discourses derived their legitimacy; about how prostitution was to be defined and resolved. (Foucault, 1972.)

Some medics and politicians regarded prostitution as a necessary safety valve for men, whose sexual needs were felt to be uncontrollable and requiring to be satisfied. From this perspective it was argued that prostitution should be state controlled to ensure that a healthy population of prostitutes would be available to service men. Others, while not actually condoning prostitution, took what they presented as a pragmatic, "neutral" position. They argued that prostitution was bound to exist, therefore the control of prostitution should be seen as a medical problem, to be tackled medically. William Acton in London (and Sanger in New York) spearheaded the medical, sanitarian approach. Acton argued:-

> However much it may be the duty of the State to leave for settlement to the individual conscience all questions of morals and religion, it can hardly be seriously contended that it is right to abandon to the care of the improvident and profligate the restraining of contagious maladies...

(Acton, 1870, in Jeffreys, 1987, p. 49.)

Some medics, however, fought against the introduction of the CD Acts. James Miller, a prominent Edinburgh surgeon and temperance orator, argued in support of the social purity stance that chastity was the only true prevention of prostitution. (Miller, 1859, p. 29.) Social purity campaigners maintained that prostitution could never be controlled by legislation - that both prostitution and its regulation upheld a sexual double standard which exploited women. This did not imply that they believed that women ought to be allowed the same sexual freedoms as men. On the contrary, they regarded women as higher beings, whose sexual standards men should be encouraged to live up to. Individual conscience, sex education of working class families (to encourage them to be more vigilant of their children's behaviour and adopt standards of supervision of young people more common in middle class families), self help and self chastity through Purity Leagues would provide the necessary strategies.

Some feminists identified strongly with the social purity movement, though not all purity campaigners were feminists. Josephine Butler argued that the "new and final solution" to the evil of male vice was to lay moral responsibility and obligation on men, every other method being "fatally incomplete". (Butler, 1875, p. 5 in Mort, 1987.) For Butler and her supporters in the Ladies National Association (LNA), prostitution and venereal disease would always be a moral, not a medical problem:-

> Because, by such a system, the path of evil is made more easy to our sons, and to the whole of the youth of England; inasmuch as a moral restraint is withdrawn the moment the State recognises, and provides convenience for, the practice of a vice which it thereby declares to be necessary and venial. Because the conditions of this disease, in the first instance, are moral, not physical. (Protest of the LNA against the CD Acts, 1870, in Jeffreys, 1987, p. 194.)

Feminists like Josephine Butler and Ellice Hopkins grasped the opportunity afforded by the controversy surrounding the CD Acts to press for change in the sexual relations between men and women - to highlight rape within marriage, incest in the family, and the sexual vulnerability of women and children. They denounced the CD Acts for depriving women of their constitutional rights, and for licensing a medical examination which amounted to a mechanical rape. The language they used was strongly Christian in tenor - their calls were to Christian morality and Christian standards in which sex would become an activity freely engaged in by men and women solely for the

16

purpose of procreation within marriage.

Clergymen opted for different sides in this debate. (Boyd, 1980.) Some established church members supported the government and the institution of the CD Acts. Others argued that venereal disease was a punishment from God for evil conduct, and therefore should not be regulated in any way. (These sentiments are mirrored in current rhetoric around HIV/AIDS.) Non-conformist churches tended to support the Ladies National Association (LNA) position that state control actually encouraged prostitution, by allowing it to continue in a more safe manner - it amounted to a "government trade in vice."[2]

Walkowitz (1980) claims that those who argued for and against the CD Acts in practice had much in common, and came from the same social grouping and background. Both groups shared a concern for regulating prostitution; and both groups, perhaps surprisingly, held similar views of women's sexuality as being essentially passive. By concentrating on the characterisation of women as vulnerable victims, they chose to ignore the economic realities which forced many women into prostitution in the first place. And yet, the social purity movement was extremely influential in furthering the cause of women's rights and women's protection. In the words of Mort (1987):-

> The purity language of outrage, like the militant tactics of suffragette politics with which it was linked, continued to provide women with a powerful weapon to challenge men. (Mort, 1987, p. 137.)

Purity organisations were highly successful in the late nineteenth century. Some organisations targeted men and boys, encouraged them to take a purity pledge for their own good and for the health of the nation. (For example, Ellice Hopkins' White Cross Army which merged in 1891 with the Church of England Purity Society to form the White Cross League.) Others focused on young women deemed to be at risk - often young women who had left home in search of employment. The Girls' Friendly Society was formed in 1874; and the Scottish Girls' Friendly Society in 1875. Their object was to "encourage loyalty and faithfulness in work and home life and self control in all things." These organisations aimed to be preventive. By providing accommodation and support to girls and young women, their moral and physical welfare would be safeguarded. For those who had already "fallen", redemption was available through reformatory institutions and rescue homes.

A victory for the social purity cause

The eventual suspension of the CD Acts in 1883 (and their repeal in 1886) clearly represented a victory for the liberal position - for the individual and private philanthropy over state control. But this did not mean that sexual morality was off the public agenda, nor that attempts to control prostitution were at an end. J.R. and D. Walkowitz (1974) suggest that following the suspension of the CD Acts, control over the lives of accused prostitutes was merely transformed to new agencies. What happened was a coming together of the agents who had been instrumental in carrying out the CD legislation (local policemen and paid informers) with the social purity campaigners, to set in motion a new system of control, organised around refuges and reformatory schools. There was in practice little distinction to be made between the regimes of the "compulsory" state Lock hospitals and the "voluntary" philanthropic refuges which took their place. Both constituted in the terms of Foucault (1977) "technologies of power", designed to create the very categories which they were set up to define and control. Mahood (1990) makes a similar point in her analysis of nineteenth century Magdalene asylums in Scotland.

With the contestation around the CD Acts over, social purity campaigners turned to a new target of concern, this time centred on the sexual behaviour of children. It was public anxiety about child prostitution and the white slave trade (the entrapment and removal of British, that is *white*, girls into brothels overseas) which was to be the final spark which led to the passing of new legislation setting the limits of permissible sexual conduct. Here we can find the beginnings of a new acceptance of a legitimate role for the state in defining and controlling sexual behaviour.

Child prostitution and the white slave trade

Child prostitution and the need to protect children from sexual activity were strong themes in the social purity discourse. Ellice Hopkins made the protection of children one of her main objectives, and toured Britain lecturing working class mothers on ways to avoid incest, and campaigning for legislation to remove children from houses where women were suspected of working as prostitutes. The notion of white slavery served to heighten public anxiety over juvenile prostitution, making connections as it did with the black slavery movement, and drawing on deep-seated racist and anti-*foreigner* attitudes.

Select Committees of the House of Lords were set up in 1881 to investigate

18

juvenile prostitution and the white slave trade, and concluded that while white slave trade allegations were largely unfounded (most British women working as prostitutes overseas had been prostitutes before they left Britain) nevertheless child prostitution was a real problem. The Industrial Schools (Amendment) Act of 1881 was passed soon afterwards, ruling that any child found to be living in the same house as a prostitute should be removed from home and taken to an industrial school. This legislation acted as a deterrent not only to prostitutes, but also to their landlords, and had the consequence of driving many prostitutes out onto the streets.

The Lords Committee at the same time recommended the raising of the age of sexual consent to 16 years (it had been raised to 13 years in 1875); giving police the power to search premises for juveniles; and raising the age of abduction for immoral purposes to 21 years. In 1883 a Criminal Law (Amendment) Bill was introduced, containing these and other proposals.

But, as with the CD Acts, the proposed legislation was not without its critics. Although social purity campaigners were in agreement that legislation was necessary, there was no agreement about what form this should take. Liberals, philanthropists and feminists had fought from the 1860s onwards against a control of prostitution which was in the hands of the police and the state alone. They were therefore unlikely to accept the legislation as it stood. James Stuart, a social purity sympathiser and Member of Parliament, illustrates this position. He attacked the Criminal Law (Amendment) Bill as it was introduced in May 1883:-

> There is too much of the police in it - I mean of absolute police action as apart from and not initiated by citizen action. We want to repress prostitution and I am convinced that cannot be done by the police, but by the action of citizens calling in the aid of the police. The moment you leave the function of repression in the hands of the police, from that moment you fail in the end you aim at, and there arises a modified system of surveillance, regulation and toleration.[3]

The Bill spent the next two years in parliament, at times debated over, at other times forgotten. When it looked as if the Bill was going to be lost forever, Josephine Butler took a surprising course of action in approaching William Stead from the Pall Mall Gazette, and enlisting his help with a plan of action aimed at changing public (and government) opinion.

"The Maiden Tribute of Modern Babylon"

The story of the "The Maiden Tribute of Modern Babylon" shows how concerns over child prostitution and white slavery were used as a means towards achieving control over the sexual behaviour of *all* men, women and children.

On the week beginning 6th July 1885, William Stead published a series of articles in the Pall Mall Gazette entitled "The Maiden Tribute of Modern Babylon", which detailed his own investigations into child prostitution in London and the story of his purchase of a thirteen year old girl, "Lily", and her removal to France. The articles were written in a sensational style, full of lurid detail of the rape of children who had been "snared, trapped, and outraged either under the influence of drugs or after a prolonged struggle in a locked room."[4]

Weeks (1981) describes the way in which the adults in these articles were presented as kinds of monsters - the aristocratic rakes who abused boys and girls (hence the last minute clause in the 1885 Act which outlawed homosexual acts); the amoral foreigners who stole children (there was a definite racist edge to this and subsequent moral panics); and the hardened mothers who sold their daughters into prostitution. The children were also caricatured, either as hapless victims or as debased, fallen young women. The level of detail and the sensational style of the articles was such that readers were outraged and titillated at the same time.

The stories caused a public outcry. On the second day of publication, W.H. Smiths, the largest retailer in the country, refused to sell any more copies of this scandalous newspaper. By the fourth day, London policemen arrested newsboys for selling obscene literature. But still the newspapers sold in their thousands, exchanging hands for ten times their normal price on the black market. The articles were published in book form, translated, and sold all over Europe and America. (Pearson, 1972; Bristow, 1977.)

The "Maiden Tribute" series was successful not because it introduced new ideas and independently created public opinion. It was successful because it exploited deep-seated fears and anxieties, and because it drew on a repertoire of feelings and representations already available in the public arena - white slave trade novels and exposes had been around for years by this time. What "the Maiden Tribute" series did was to escalate a threat already known and understood. William Stead, editor of the Pall Mall Gazette, admitted that he "only struck the match that fired a charged mine of enthusiasm".[5] (See Watney, 1987, for a critique of conventional representations of moral panics. He argues that a particular moral panic marks the site of the current front line in ideological struggles.)

Public protest forced the interim conservative government to carry out its own investigations into Stead's allegations. These enquiries confirmed the existence of the white slave trade, but questioned its extent. Protest meetings continued throughout Britain, and a petition with 393,000 signatures was presented to Parliament. The Criminal Law (Amendment) Act was hurriedly passed on 14th August 1885.

The Criminal Law (Amendment) Act - a compromise solution

The main provisions of the Criminal Law (Amendment) Act of 1885 were as follows:-

1   It became an offence to procure a woman under 21 years of age for prostitution - those found guilty were liable to a prison sentence of not less than two years;
2   The age of sexual consent was raised from 13 to 16 years;
3   Anyone who detained a women or a girl for the purposes of unlawful sex, in any brothel or other premises was guilty of an offence;
4   Any male found committing homosexual acts in private or public could be sent to prison for up to two years;
5   Financial penalties or imprisonment were imposed on anyone found guilty of keeping, managing, assisting, owning or renting out premises used as a brothel, or for the purposes of prostitution.

The passing of the Criminal Law (Amendment) Act and the formation of the NVA represents a deliberate compromise - a compromise between those who wished to see prostitution regulated and controlled, and those who believed that regulation was a matter for the individual, not the state; and a compromise between those who had fought for and against the imposition of the CD Acts. The NVA's expressed purpose was to be the main agency which would undertake private prosecutions and alert the police to infringements of the new law. This was not aimed at extending the effectiveness of the law. It illustrated instead the liberal and feminist position.

It would be wrong, however, to characterise the Criminal Law (Amendment) Act as a liberal Act. The circumstances which led to its passing were anything but liberal minded, and its consequences were cruel and repressive. In the desperate need to force a change of law, the liberal/personal rights strand of the social purity discourse was lost completely. "The Maiden Tribute" revelations were largely manufactured -

21

the problem of juvenile prostitution in London never reached the extent of Stead's allegations. And the purchase of "Lily" (Eliza Armstrong) was as seedy and unpleasant as any of the crimes which the Pall Mall Gazette articles described. Eliza's mother had not sold her daughter into prostitution as the stories alleged. Instead, she was told that her daughter was going into domestic service. Eliza was then forcibly examined to check her virginity, and smuggled over to France where she was held in a room. Stead was subsequently sentenced to six months' imprisonment for the abduction of Eliza Armstrong.[6]

The Criminal Law (Amendment) Act has been described overall as "a particularly nasty and pernicious piece of omnibus legislation." (Walkowitz, 1982.) Following the passing of the Act, prostitutes found themselves increasingly vulnerable and under attack, on the streets rather than in the comparative safety of brothels or rented rooms; male homosexuals were charged with indecent behaviour and imprisoned in great numbers. (There is some debate about why this anti-homosexual clause was introduced and accepted at the last minute. See Smith, 1976 and Weeks, 1981.)

Legislation passed a few years later in 1889 regarding the physical abuse of children by their parents followed the same principle of voluntary enforcement and private prosecution. New voluntary organisations - the National Society for the Prevention of Cruelty to Children (NSPCC) for England, Wales and Ireland, and the Scottish National Society for the Prevention of Cruelty to Children (SNSPCC) - were set up to be the principal agencies for investigating and prosecuting parents in cases of child abuse by parents. (Behlmer, 1982.)

Donzelot's analysis of the role of philanthropy is useful here. He identifies the emergence in the nineteenth century of a new set of discourses whose common thread was a concern for the family, and a new site of activity and a new conceptual space which he terms "the social". Philanthropy (and later social work) developed not as an apolitical, private intervention into social problems, but a "deliberately depoliticising strategy for establishing public services at sensitive points midway between private initiative and the state." (Donzelot, 1980, p. 55.)

There can be few points more sensitive than the NVA's attempts to change the sexual behaviour of men, women and children. The NVA hoped that by holding onto the reins of the vigilance discourse it would retain control over state intervention in family life. At the same time, it conceded that the state did now have a role in monitoring private lives and behaviour. What we see increasingly throughout the twentieth century is a steady incorporation of social work activity into the welfare state. Voluntary agencies which had operated at Donzelot's "midway point" have become increasingly a constituent part of state welfare provision. (See Chapter Seven.)

The National Vigilance Association

The National Vigilance Association (NVA) was launched at a public meeting in London one week after the passing of the Criminal Law (Amendment) Act. The NVA had two main aims - to ensure that the new legislation was enforced, and to press for further legislation "to repress criminal vice and public immorality" if deemed necessary.[7] The next few years were undoubtedly the high point in the vigilance movement. New branches of the NVA opened up across Britain. Lecture tours and speeches by leading purity figures encouraged the growth of NVA branches at local level throughout Britain, so that by 1888 there were 300 affiliated groups. But not all these groups survived. Many local committees collapsed, especially after the initial excitement had evaporated. (Bristow, 1977.)

The NVA had no easy consensus to rely on. Even at the beginning, it was fraught with internal disagreements between individuals and groups. In the years which followed its formation, it relied on a strategy of periodic well-orchestrated public campaigns centred on different vigilance concerns (prostitution, the white slave trade, the age of sexual consent, obscenity and pornography, sexual abuse of children) as a means towards securing its support and its position. Some of these campaigns had a high measure of success - for example, thanks in large part to NVA activity, incest was criminalised for the first time in England and Wales in 1908. Other campaigns were less successful. The age of sexual consent was never raised to eighteen years, or even twenty one years, in line with NVA recommendations.

Gorham (1978) cites the age of consent controversy as an example of her view that many of the vigilance reformers did not fully understand either their own motives or the nature of the problem which they were attempting to confronts. NVA supporters who pushed for the extension of the age of consent to twenty one years, did so based on their view that girls and young women were defenceless creatures who required supervision and surveillance. But there were huge class differences between the experiences of working class children (who routinely left home to find work, aged twelve or thirteen years) and the sheltered lives of middle class children. The NVA's aims were therefore about more than changing the sexual behaviour of men and women in general. They were also about transforming codes of conduct of working class families to match those of "desirable", bourgeois families.

Although the NVA was a national organisation, engaged in national and

23

international campaigns, each branch operated as a separate unit with its own management and independent financial structure. The NVA based in London was in fact the London NVA, at the same time as being the headquarters of a national body. This led to a high level of autonomy amongst NVA branches, and a degree of difference in branch priorities. By examining in some detail the activities of one branch of the NVA - the NVA of Scotland (Eastern Division) - we can see more clearly the vigilance discourse being worked out, in all its contradictions. What we have here is a picture of one NVA group struggling to hold onto and develop the vigilance cause, in the face of internal uncertainties and external competition from other social purity organisations.

The NVA of Scotland (Eastern Division)

The NVA of Scotland (Eastern Division) was established in 1911 in Edinburgh in response to yet another white slave trade furore, this time set in motion by NVA Secretary William Coote's world-wide campaign to tackle the "growing problem" of traffic in women and girls to brothels overseas. (Coote, 1910.) The first branch in Scotland opened in Glasgow in 1910, then the Eastern Division, covering the east of Scotland from the Borders right up to Orkney began in 1911. (Later NVA branches also became established in Perth and in Aberdeen.)

Following a similar pattern to the NVA in London, the NVA (Eastern Division) reflected a mix in its membership and supporters, and included prominent feminists (Lady Frances Balfour and Dr Elsie Inglis); leading churchmen (Rev. Robert Drummond and Canon Albert Laurie); influential doctors, lawyers, politicians, and wives and daughters of the Edinburgh upper classes. Its purpose, as I have stated, was to protect women and girls from outrage, abduction and prostitution, and from the cruelty of the white slave trade. This "protection" of women and girls was to be achieved by campaigning and activity across a number of fronts, as the breadth of the NVA's work illustrates. This approach was summed up in a speech by the Lord Provost of Edinburgh, Sir Alexander Stevenson, in 1928. He asserted that Edinburgh was becoming:-

> .... not only a healthier, but a purer place to live, as public statistics show. Punishment, restriction, prevention and moral suasion are all doing their part in that great improvement.[8]

Punishment, restriction, prevention and moral suasion were indeed all essential parts of the vigilance strategy. "*Punishment*", as the measures detailed in the 1885 Act make clear, was mainly focused on the harassment of brothel keepers and pimps (and gay men), rather than on prostitutes themselves, who were to be controlled more through "restriction" and "moral suasion" rather than by "punishment". Nevertheless, as I have said already, prosecutions of brothel keepers and landlords who rented rooms to women working as prostitutes had a serious impact on prostitutes, who found themselves homeless and unable to find alternative accommodation. (And this legislation came on top of the 1881 Industrial Schools Act, which I have already described as increasing women's homelessness, at the same time as leading to their children being removed from home.)

The NVA was not content to let existing legislation stand. Reading agency records of the NVA in London and in Edinburgh there is always the sense that "things are getting worse", so that more stringent legislation is necessary. A central strand of NVA activity throughout Britain centred on pressure for further legislation on the control of prostitution. In 1912 a second Criminal Law (Amendment) Act was passed, extending the powers of the 1885 Act by giving courts discretionary powers to whip as well as imprison men convicted of procuring or living off the earnings of prostitutes. Finally in 1922 a third Act was passed, lengthening to nine months the period during which a victim of sexual assault could lodge a complaint, and limiting the "reasonable cause to believe" defence to men of twenty three years or younger. (This clause had allowed male defendants to claim that they believed that a girl in a sexual assault case was over sixteen years of age.) NVA campaigners were never able to completely get rid of this hated "escape clause", just as they were never able to raise the age of sexual consent further in line with NVA policy.

At the local level, NVA workers worked hard to ensure that anti-prostitution legislation was effectively carried out. They regularly investigated brothels, dance halls and "dangerous houses", removing young women and children thought to be at risk, and alerting the police to infringements of the new legislation. The relationship between the local police and NVA workers in Edinburgh seems to have been co-operative. Police followed up on "tip-offs" from the NVA, and NVA staff looked into complaints from members of the public and from the police. Not all cities enjoyed such a good working relationship with the NVA. Ware (1969) notes that in some areas police and authorities did not want brothels closed down, believing that it was better that vice was kept "well in order". (Ware, 1969, p. 432.)

There is an important point here for an understanding of the vigilance discourse. Prostitution and its control remained a contentious, difficult area even for NVA supporters, just as it had been for those fighting for and against the Contagious Diseases Acts fifty years and more earlier. During the First World War, NVA members in Edinburgh were split 50-50 on a proposal that they should join the campaign for the withdrawal of the 40D Defence of the Realm (DORA) Regulations - regulations which were strongly reminiscent of the CD Acts, and which stipulated that women having sex with soldiers should be compulsorally examined for venereal disease.[9] They did however agree that same year to send two delegates in support of the Women's Freedom League deputation to Parliament, protesting against two Bills on the State Regulation of Vice.[10] In 1929, members set up a sub-committee and subsequently supported the national NVA's stance on the Street Offences Report.[11] But, as in the First World War, the Committee was unable to reach agreement on a proposal for the repeal of Regulation 33B (which allowed for the notification and examination of women for venereal disease) during the Second World War.[12] These examples show that while prostitution was regarded as a problem, and one which merited a measure of control and "punishment", there was no simple consensus about how this should be achieved.

"Restriction" can be found in the NVA's anti-pornography campaigns - checking films, plays and pantomimes for obscenity; pressing for the removal of books, prints and postcards. The NVA also joined in the campaign to restrict the sale of what were called "rubber goods" through magazines - contraceptive devices. During the early 1930s the NVA played a major part in a city wide Cinema Enquiry, ensuring that children under the age of sixteen years were not being allowed to view what were regarded as "unsuitable" films. It was believed that restricting the access of people (and children in particular) to sexual materials would reduce the likelihood of their being corrupted by those materials. Campaigns such as this led to the setting up of a certification system for films, which limits certain films for adult viewing only. Similar arguments are being waged today around children watching unsuitable home videos, just as television's effect on children was of central concern in the 1960s and 1970s.

"Restriction" went hand in hand with *"prevention"*, an idea which pervades all the work of the NVA. This was prevention in terms of preventing the sexual exploitation of women and girls; preventing them from being ensnared into "white slavery"; preventing rescued prostitutes from going back into prostitution; preventing unmarried mothers from having a second illegitimate child. This is very different from the post 1968 Social Work (Scotland) Act notion of prevention, which conceptualised prevention in terms of preventing family breakdown and reception into care. Instead, here prevention was often achieved by removing a child or young person from home, and placing them in a residential home or school, or live-in work situation where they would be prevented from having contact with the "bad" influences of the past.

"Prevention" and *"restriction"* were achieved through the agency's strong

public presence. What is distinctive about the early vigilance work is that this was very public work - it happened on the streets, in the meeting-places, in the public arena. In spite of the fact that the subject of prostitution and sexuality itself was highly controversial, middle and upper-class women and men were prepared to stand out in the public gaze and engage in what was potentially dangerous work - dangerous to their reputations and sometimes dangerous to their persons.

The idea of a public presence is very strong in the agency literature. The 1929 Annual Report notes:-

> The very presence of a Vigilance representative every evening in the station keeps away the undesirable characters who at one time found these places veritable hunting grounds."[13]

The "hunting grounds" were many and varied. Workers (and on occasions committee members) policed public parks used by courting couples and specifically, homosexual men[14], and they patrolled the streets, the bus and railway stations and the docks, acting as a physical preventive to immoral conduct. Sometimes the presence of an NVA representative (wearing NVA hat and large metal badge) was seen as sufficient deterrent. At other times workers took direct action, approaching and addressing couples and unaccompanied women, and boarding ships in the docks to search for women.

It was not always women who were seen as potential victims requiring protection. During World War One, the outdoor worker patrolled outside the barracks in Edinburgh to prevent soldiers being molested by women, reflecting the new concern about the threat of "amateur prostitutes." (Bland and Mort, 1984.) In the years between the two World Wars, the NVA undertook a major piece of preventive work with men. Between 1931 and 1939, 20,000 sailors were accommodated in church halls throughout Edinburgh while the Home Fleet was stationed in South Queensferry for the autumn. This service was in part a humanitarian response to people in need - preventing men from being forced to sleep on the streets. It was also designed to keep men out of the clutches of prostitutes, and safe for their wives at home.[15]

The NVA was not the only agency engaged in street patrolling in Edinburgh at this time. A large number of "benevolent" organisations - churches and evangelical groups as well as the NVA employed women to patrol the streets and survey behaviour (for example, Young Women's Christian Association, Girls' Friendly Society, plus many Church Mission groups). Manuals were published which described what to look out for - the girl who did not seem to

27

welcome the attentions of a man, the men who were cruising about looking for girls. There was even competition at times for control of the streets. In 1913, the NVA worker investigated a report of a woman dressed as a nurse accosting girls in Princes Street. (The picture of a nurse was a typical white slave trade representation of a way of duping innocent girls.) This "nurse" was later found to be a worker from the Baptist Church in Rose Street.[16]

"Moral suasion" was the preferred approach in the individual work with women. Most "individual cases" (a term which appears in the earliest records) were young women aged between 16 and 23 years, though a substantial number were under 16 years of age (for example the 12 year old in 1913 who was recorded as "thoroughly bad and suffering from disease.")[17] A few were older, for example a 28 year old pregnant woman from Inverness was helped in 1914.[18] While principal clients were women, men were not forgotten. When parents of runaway girls were contacted, both parents were expected to be involved in discussions. When a girl reported sexual abuse, workers attempted to trace "the man who had put the girl wrong."[19] In cases of illegitimate pregnancy, workers pursued putative fathers for the payment of "aliment" (maintenance) towards the cost of boarding-out the child, or of a children's home. (This was a service which the agency continued to carry out on behalf of single parents until the 1960s when new social security arrangements made this no longer necessary.) Occasionally, boys were regarded as being in moral danger and became agency cases, for example in 1938 a 14 year old boy who had got to know "older and very undesirable friends" was sent to live on a farm.[20]

The young women who sought help from the NVA, or were referred to the NVA by parents or court or other voluntary or public bodies (including the workhouse, the Children's Shelter, and the police) came to the NVA primarily because they were in difficulty. They were unemployed; they were homeless or living in "dangerous surroundings" (in a house suspected of being a brothel, or in a house where the male householder was known to be violent or abusive); they had no money and no means of support. Some had run away from home, from employers and from institutions, and some had suffered sexual abuse or assault. Some were in a short term predicament. They had missed their last bus or train home, or had ran out of money. Others were pregnant, or had recently had an illegitimate baby - these were the cases which were to increasingly take up the time of the NVA workers. Occasionally, women who were prostitutes were helped, but only on the strict understanding that they should not "return to their former lives".

The NVA's task varied according to the nature of the case. Some women were given temporary accommodation, a loan of cash, or were accompanied back home again, or sometimes to a boat from where they would emigrate to start a new life in north America or Australia. Others were found work (often domestic service or hospital work), lodgings, and where necessary, a boarding out placement for their babies. Many were taken to institutions to be re-educated morally and spiritually and to learn a useful trade (again, domestic service and laundry work featured prominently.)

Another place where "moral suasion" was much in evidence was court work. NVA workers regularly attended police and sheriff courts to assist young women and act as probation officers when requested.[21] The deployment of probation workers from voluntary agencies continued far longer in Edinburgh than in other cities. After the Probation of Offenders Act in 1931, the Lord Provost of Edinburgh decided not to appoint salaried officers "in view of the unqualified success of the voluntary probation system presently in operation." The last agency record of any involvement of the NVA in Edinburgh in probation work is 1944. In 1947, local authority statutory provision of probation work began.

"Moral suasion" was not targeted only as individual cases however. The NVA mounted a hard-fought campaign to get sex education on the public agenda. This was not sex education in terms of advice to young people on how to have safe sex, but sex education which railed against the dangers and evils of extra-marital sex. NVA supporters pressed school boards in 1913 and 1914 (with no success) to introduce sex education in schools, and at the same time carried out its own campaign of public education. Leaflets to men, women and girls were sold in their thousands at meetings and rallies.

Over and above these self-evidently vigilance activities, the NVA in Edinburgh undertook a wide variety of activity which was not vigilance in the narrow sense of social purity, but what is much more accurately described as *women's issues*, and perhaps even women's rights. Members fought for better lighting in parks and streets (1912); for the provision of public toilets for women (1913); for the appointment of women doctors to the courts (1916 and 1924); and carried out a protracted and hard fought struggle from 1914 until the early 1940s to get police women appointed in Edinburgh. These extra activities illustrate the breadth of the vigilance discourse. Unlike the social purity movement, the vigilance movement was always a diverse grouping, which engaged in a wide range of activities. This is important for an understanding of the complexities and contradictions which existed within the vigilance discourse, from its beginnings right up to today.

The vigilance discourse in decline

The NVA at national level was in serious difficulties even as early as the

1920s. The Association had initiated prosecutions in respect of indecent advertising, the music halls, prostitution and pornography. But because it was never successful in recouping from the government the costs of private prosecutions, there was soon no money left to pursue further prosecutions. (Mort, 1987.) The shaky compromise reached over prostitution and its control in 1885 did not last either. The agency found it itself unable to attract new supporters, and some original supporters (like Josephine Butler) left the NVA, unable to reconcile themselves with what they saw as an increasingly repressive approach towards prostitution.

The result was that the vigilance discourse shattered, and vigilance work became dispersed. Gradually the international work was subsumed by the United Nations. At the same time, new social purity organisations grew up, organisations which had little interest in feminist ideas and which were much more concerned to express a new commitment to physical, moral and racial health - what Bland and Mort (1984) refer to as a new "medico-moral coalition." And statutory authorities (principally the police and legal authorities) increasingly assumed responsibility for prostitution and its management and control.

In 1952, the NVA nationally was forced by a financial crisis to undertake a merger between its two remaining branches of vigilance activity, the NVA and the British National Committee, under the new title of the British Vigilance Association (BVA). The much reduced BVA during the 1950s and 1960s concentrated its activities on lobbying government over a number of different campaigns. It engaged in a lengthy battle to encourage the government to introduce legislation enforcing the licensing of commercial Employment Agencies. It publicised the plight of Irish girls in Britain, who had been promised work by agencies and then found themselves without work or accommodation. It also campaigned for legislation on "horror comics", resulting in the Children and Young Persons (Harmful Publications) Act of 1955, and presented evidence on prostitution to the Wolfenden committee - the Departmental Enquiry on Homosexuality and Prostitution. Throughout the 1960s, the BVA pushed for legislation to raise the minimum age permissible for au pairs to seventeen years of age; for a European au pair convention; and for the passing of a new Street Offences Act which would target men as well as women for prosecution. The BVA also continued to operate kiosks for travellers at Victoria and Liverpool Street Stations in London. Financial difficulties remained, however, and the BVA was finally wound up at an Extraordinary General Meeting on 6 December 1971.

The NVA (Eastern Division) continued beyond this point, and still exists today. But its continuance was achieved only because the agency chose to move away from vigilance concerns - away from public work in the streets and in the public arena towards work which was centred on the private world of the individual and the family. It was the individual work with cases which became the main growth point within the agency's work, as increasingly the rooting out of prostitution and immorality was left to the new experts in the situation - the police and the medical authorities. The principal Object in 1946 became "to advise and befriend women and children by means of individual casework."[22]

This was not a transformation which happened overnight. Old and new discourses existed side by side and at times in contradiction with one another for many years. The local branch continued to send delegates to British National Committee meetings in London right up to the early 1950s. Although patrolling and street surveillance was wound up in the 1930s and 1940s, during the Second World War a new joint initiative between the NVA, local YWCA, national YWCA and Travellers' Aid Society established a kiosk for women travellers at Waverley Station in Edinburgh. This was closed in 1946 when two women police officers were appointed to work at the station. (But the NVA did not give up helping travellers completely at this time. The agency took referrals from the NVA in London and from other organisations who informed them of women coming to Edinburgh seeking work or accommodation until 1958 when this service was ended.) Also during the war, members campaigned for greater supervision in Air Raid Shelters, and investigated the living conditions of Land Army girls in Scotland. But increasingly, the Association displayed discomfort at its vigilance origins, usually expressed in attempts to change the name of the organisation. After years of debate about the name, in 1941 the Association transposed its two titles and became The International Guild of Service for Women, with a subtitle The National Vigilance Association (Eastern Division).

The shift away from vigilance work can be seen in the context of what Chambers (1959) describes as a "squeeze" which was affecting all moral welfare workers throughout Britain after the Second World War and taking over the moral welfare field (in which vigilance work played such a significant role). Almoners and medical social workers took over responsibility for follow-up work connected with venereal disease; the Youth Service developed initiatives in preventive work; Health Visitors assisted with maternity provisions; and of course statutory Probation Officers replaced voluntary ones. Moral welfare workers found their role more strictly defined than ever before, and were obliged to look for new directions in their work.

The break with the vigilance work in Edinburgh came in the period after the resignation of the long serving Organising Secretary in 1954. In 1958, with the appointment of a new Director the agency set itself the task of building its professional social work image, and leaving behind "the NVA, whose more militant attitude towards sin and the fallen we are glad to forget."[23] In 1962, the re-named subtitle "formerly NVA" was finally removed from the agency's name.

Present day vigilance discourse

What of the vigilance discourse? Was it lost forever with the demise of the NVA? I believe that although the vigilance movement as such has disappeared, vigilance ideas and vigilance debates persist in the public domain today, with wide reaching implications for the task of social work.

The first important point is that state intervention in the private lives of individuals remains a contentious issue. The right to prohibit, control, and intervene in matters of private sexual behaviour continues to be open to debate. Although at one level the argument about the state's right to intervene may seem to be won (for example, in the establishment of statutory duties carried out by social workers in respect of child protection) the balance between individual and statutory rights, between private and public behaviour, continues to be negotiated with and fought over. This debate has been waged again in connection with the sexual abuse of children, when parents in Cleveland and later in Orkney accused the statutory authorities of taking unnecessary, punitive and damaging action in removing children who were suspected of having been sexually abused from their homes. The present "compromise solution" (as laid out in the Children Act 1989 and in the White Paper, *Scotland's Children*) accepts the right for intervention in families' lives, but overlays this with an obligation to respect the rights of parents. Parton (1991) argues that social work has a key mediating role here, mediating between the public and the private, the state and the family. This exactly parallels the role which the nineteenth century NVA (and NSPCC/ SNSPCC) sought to hold, acting as a midway point between the individual and the state, and setting limits on the power of both. (Donzelot, 1980.)

Just as private/public morality remains a contested area, so does prostitution and its control. I have argued that consensus over prostitution was only achieved for a brief moment in time, at the end of a long, hard fought campaign which reached a head with the "Maiden Tribute" allegations. Controversy remains today about prostitution and how it should be dealt with. Some police authorities (like Lothian and Borders) choose to take a low key approach, resulting in relatively small numbers of women being convicted for soliciting. Others (like Strathclyde) take a much more proactive approach, seeking out and charging women prostitutes.

Feminists today, as in the nineteenth century, find it impossible to reach agreement on a feminist response to prostitution. While feminists on one side call for the decriminalisation of prostitution, and for the reformulation of prostitution as "sex work" and a legitimate part of the service industry, others maintain that prostitution will always degrade women, and allow patriarchal systems and attitudes to survive and flourish. (Alexander, 1988; Shrage, 1989.)

Feminists are equally divided on the issue of pornography. Pornography can be regarded as an assault on women, which should therefore always be controlled, or it may be argued that pornography (like prostitution) sets out to make male domination more acceptable - it erotises that domination. On the other hand, some feminists highlight the damaging effects of censorship in terms of freedom of speech and civil liberties, and therefore argue against legal controls on pornography. (Smart, 1989; Segal and McIntosh, 1992.)

Vigilance-type exposes and vigilance-style campaigns have continued to emerge at various moments, long after the formal vigilance movement has collapsed. Throughout the 1970s, 1980s and into the 1990s, issues such as teenage sexuality, immorality, contraception, abortion, and unmarried motherhood have continued to receive prominent press attention. And "white slave trade" stories have continued to fascinate the media - stories of young women and children forced to take part in pornographic videos,[24] or of British dancers ensnared into brothels overseas. More popular in recent years have been the "black slave trade" stories - allegations that women from the Third World (South America, the Middle East, and now Eastern Europe) are being trapped into prostitution for the benefit of wealthy white foreigners. Young children are again seen to be most at risk here, highly prized because of presumed lower incidence of sexually transmitted diseases. This media coverage follows the familiar "Maiden Tribute" pattern of titillating at the same time as shocking the reader or viewer, with a strong underlying message that action must be taken to prevent further abuse. At the same time women and children are confirmed as being vulnerable, passive victims, in need of protection.

Recent popular press attention has turned to the establishment of new social purity organisations which have grown up in the context of a deeply conservative, "pro-family" movement in the United States. Echoing Ellice Hopkins' purity pledges, American teenagers are joining a "True Love Waits" programme, and pledging to remain virgins until marriage.[25] This development stands in marked contrast to the reality that most of the early social purity movement's aims cannot be said to have been successful. Rising divorce figures and a steady increase in children born outside marriage suggests that men's sexual behaviour has not risen to that of women. In fact

33

from a social purity standpoint, the reverse is true - that women from the 1960s onwards, thanks to the wider availability of contraception and abortion, have been able to "lower" their standards to those of men.

It is the rise of HIV/AIDS which has brought vigilance themes to prominence from the 1980s onwards. Mort (1987) argues that the popular media has played a critical role in shaping opinion over AIDS, setting the boundaries for debate, identifying the problem and its potential solutions. Homosexuals, prostitutes and drug users are all blamed for spreading the disease. Tales of sexual outrage are never isolated cases - they must be understood in their wider social and political vocabulary:-

> AIDS has come to occupy a distinctive place on the ideological repertoire of the moral right ... More and more, "sexual undesirables" have been twinned with the "socially undesirable." (Mort, 1987, p. 214.)

Concern for the spread of HIV/AIDS has led to the establishment of a new generation of organisations taking part in street work with female and male prostitutes. "Outreach work" has replaced the "outdoor work" of the NVA, but the task remains the same, to go out onto the streets and to get to know and befriend prostitutes. In Edinburgh there are now three such organisations, two targeted at women prostitutes and one at men ("rent boys"). Of course there are key differences in approach and style between this work and the work of the NVA. The outreach workers today see their work in terms of health promotion. They are interested in saving bodies, not souls. They accept that prostitution is a chosen activity, and offer condoms, medical examinations for all sexually transmitted diseases, and counselling on a wide range of problems. Their basic philosophy is underpinned by ideas of self help and empowerment, rather than paternalistic, judgmental ideas about rescue and penitence.[26]

I believe however that there is a connection between outreach projects today and outdoor work from the early twentieth century. It was agitation around the spread of venereal disease which led to the focus on women prostitutes as people in need of support and control. Today it is the spread of HIV/AIDS which has again put prostitution in the public gaze. And just as soldiers were largely ignored by the CD Acts, so it is women, not men who use prostitutes, whose behaviour is under scrutiny. At the same time, many of the projects which have emerged in recent years have their roots in Christian philanthropy. The first prostitution project in Edinburgh was begun by the Church of Scotland and funded by the Women's Guild to mark its centenary. Statutory social work agencies find it more difficult to work out their own stance on prostitution. Although Children and Families' social workers and Criminal Justice social workers undoubtedly carry cases in which prostitution plays a major part, Lothian Region Social Work Department has no policy on prostitution.[27]   Birmingham Social Services Department serves as another illustration.   A recent research study on juvenile prostitution was shelved as too controversial to be published.[28]

If prostitution is "too hot to handle", the same cannot be said for the sexual abuse of children.   While the 1970s has been described as the period when child abuse was "re-discovered", the 1980s brought child sexual abuse to the top of the public agenda.   (Parton, 1991.)   Social workers today are handling increasing numbers of cases of child sexual abuse.   Children's Hearings statistics bear this out.[29]   As the number of children referred to the Reporter in Lothian Region on the grounds of an offence has declined steadily since 1975, so the number of children where sexual abuse is suspected or known has increased dramatically.   Children referred under Section 32(2)b - "falling into bad associations or exposed to moral danger" - has increased from seventeen in 1976 to eighty one in 1993.   Figures are also rising under other categories referring to child abuse and neglect - Section 32(2)c, d, and dd - and here the underlying concern is often sexual abuse.[30]

One of the major reasons for this increase is not that more children are being sexually abused (which is clearly impossible to ascertain) but that more children are coming forward and talking about the abuse.   High profile campaigns have set out to publicise sexual abuse, and to urge victims to come forward for help.   On a national level, Childline was set up in 1987, offering a nation wide telephone counselling service to children who were being, or had been abused.   This has been extended to offer a specific service to children in residential schools.   In addition, new self help organisations (such as Who Cares Scotland) have acted as a mouth piece and support for children in, or leaving local authority care.

More locally, two campaigns are worthy of note.   Edinburgh City Council Women's Committee launched a highly controversial poster campaign in November 1992 aimed at highlighting men's violence (physical, sexual and emotional) to women and children in the family.   The Zero Tolerance campaign promoted the slogan "There's no excuse" on buses, in libraries and on public streets, and has been extended to cities throughout Britain.   This is the kind of sex education/ preventive work which the NVA would have been proud to have been associated with, and picks up themes which the NVA was publicising in its own meetings and leaflet distribution eighty years earlier.

Another local initiative, the Child Abuse Prevention Programme, is a sex education programme with a difference, targeted at children in Primary Schools in Lothian Region.   Lothian and Borders Police have come together with the Education Department to set up a training programme for all children based on the principle of personal safety, in which children are encouraged to share their feelings and talk about behaviours they find acceptable and unacceptable. The programme has been so successful that Children's Hearing Reporters can pinpoint a direct increase in referrals to the Hearing system, after children have come through the programme, and found the courage to talk to teachers, youth workers and social workers about alleged abuse.[31]

Lothian and Borders Police are also working co-operatively with the Social Work Department on "vigilance" concerns. In 1988 the police authority set up for the first time in Edinburgh city a Women and Child Unit, now extended to all Lothian and Borders areas. Its purpose is to work with all cases associated with rape, incest, sexual assault, child abuse, and child sexual abuse. The Women and Child Unit began as a women's organisation, emerging out of criticism of the police handling of rape cases, and after years of campaigning by Rape Crisis. Today eighty per cent of its work is with children, and here police officers carry out interviews on a joint basis with social workers, and police officers and social workers undergo joint training in the management of child abuse.[32]

From this brief introduction, we can see that the vigilance discourse operates across a number of different sites, statutory and voluntary. Social work, police, education, health service, local government, voluntary organisations, media and pressure groups all participate in what might be called vigilance work. This is one of the major differences between the vigilance movement at the turn of the century and today. Issues such as pornography, contraception, abortion, censorship, prostitution, child sexual abuse and rape are all tackled separately by often opposing groups, and attempts to make links between issues, for example between pornographic literature/ films and sexual assaults on women, have not had much success. Smart (1981) suggests that the reasons for this failure lie in the fact that the moral discourse on sexuality has been largely superseded by a legal discourse, often expressed in medical terms, with medical experts and legal rulings dictating terms of reference and parameters of permissible behaviour. While this may be an accurate reflection of the position up to the late 1970s, I believe that what we are seeing today is a much greater acceptance of the feminist/vigilance discourse across a wide spectrum of society. Violence against women is no longer dismissed as a domestic affair; sexual abuse of children is no longer perceived as the child's "fault" - though there are exceptions to this generalisation. What we can see today is public acceptance of a more explicit presentation of sex, accompanied by greater public awareness of, and acceptance of the feminist/vigilance standpoint on sexual abuse. Sexual behaviour is increasingly regulated and controlled, even in our seemingly more liberal, permissive society. (Foucault, 1979.)

One of the most far reaching consequences of the vigilance discourse has been the statutory definition of women and girls as persons in need of special protection and special surveillance, thus legitimating in law what was essentially a moral position. Today women within the criminal justice system are still treated differently to men. They are likely to be imprisoned for less serious offences, and locked up for longer periods. Decisions to lock women up or not tend to be based on their status as good or bad wives and mothers, rather than the nature of the offences committed. (Carlen, 1983 and 1985; Smart and Smart, 1978.) The same is true for girls. Girls coming before juvenile courts and children's hearings are more likely than boys to be there for reasons which have to do with their sexual behaviour - they are defined as being "in moral danger". Once identified as such, they are more likely to be removed from home, again for their protection and control. (Campbell, 1981; Casburn, 1979; Gelsthorpe, 1987.) The reasons for such differential treatment are most likely to be expressed in psychological or pseudo medical language, but the underlying sentiments are firmly moral ones.

Summary

This chapter has been about a beginning and an ending - about the beginning of a new acceptance of a role for the state in the private world of sexuality, and about the eclipse of the vigilance movement. The state's entry into the private realm of sexuality and family life was at first very cautious. The initiatives came from feminists and social purists, not the government. But as the vigilance movement was prepared to use the law to achieve its demands, so what had been defined as private and moral concerns became legalised and institutionalised.

Although the vigilance movement itself has ended, feminist/vigilance/social purity issues and concerns have been taken up across a wide public spectrum, fuelled by periodic explosions of media interest in sexual behaviour, and currently centred on child sexual abuse and HIV/AIDS. These modern day vigilance campaigns continue to play an influential role in affirming and maintaining the parameters for our professional and common sense views on the "correct" sexual behaviour of men, women and children. And social work remains one of the principal sites through which and in which the battle to control sexual behaviour is fought.

Notes

1. First Object of NVA (Eastern Division), Annual Report, 1917 (the earliest annual report still surviving in the agency).
2. LNA (1907), "The Ladies National Association. What it is and Why it is still Needed", re-printed in Jeffreys (1987), pp. 191-193.
3. James Stuart writing to Samuel Smith, 8 July, 1884, re-printed in Bristow 1977) p. 93.
4. *Pall Mall Gazette*, 6 July 1885, p. 1.
5. *Pall Mall Gazette*, 22 August 1885, p. 15.
6. Stead was charged because he had not sought permission from Eliza's father. When it later emerged that Eliza's parents were not married and that she was illegitimate, Stead was freed because the father's consent had never been necessary.
7. Resolution published in *The Sentinel*, 1885, p. 475.
8. Reported in *Vigilance Record*, December 1928.
9. Executive Committee minutes, 21-04-18.
10. Executive Committee minutes, 07-11-18.
11. Executive Committee minutes, 19-02-29.
12. Executive Committee minutes, 15-10-43.
13. Annual Report, 1929.
14. Executive Committee minutes, 1912.
15. Interview, 17-07-90.
16. Ladies Committee minutes, 26-02-13.
17. Ladies Committee minutes, 06-06-13.
18. Ladies Committee minutes, 06-05-14.
19. Ladies Committee minutes, 06-06-13.
20. Annual Report, 1938, p. 12.
21. The Probation of Offenders Act (1907) enabled courts throughout the United Kingdom to appoint probation officers who would carry out the new Probation Orders. Most of these Officers in Scotland were Church of Scotland Police Court Missionaries, but other organisations, like the NVA, also provided named Officers. The Criminal Justice Act (1925) provided for the establishment of a salaried Probation Service in England and Wales; Scotland did enact similar legislation until the Probation of Offenders (1931) Scotland Act. Even after the passing of these Acts, there was a high level of local variation. (King, 1964).
22. Annual Report, 1946.
23. Annual Report, 1957.
24. *Daily Record*, 08-02-90.
25. *Sunday Mail*, 08-05-94.

Continued

26. Interview, 26-05-94.
27. Correspondence with Regional Co-ordinator for Child Abuse, Lothian Region Social Work Department, 01-06-94.
28. Correspondence with Policy Performance Review Manager, Birmingham Social Service Department.
29. Lothian Regional Council, Annual Report, The Children's Hearing System in the Lothian Region, May 1992 to May 1993.
30. Interview with Regional Reporter, 27-04-94.
31. Interview with Regional Reporter, 27-04-94.
32. Interview with Sergeant at Women and Child Unit, 26-05-94.

3 Secularisation and social work

Introduction

This chapter explores the place of moral and Christian ideas and practices within the values, knowledge base and day to day interventions of social work, and argues that Christian voices of morality and service continue to play a significant part in social work discourse today. Although the Christian tradition in Family Care (with its roots in highly religious moral welfare work) is likely to be stronger than in some other social work settings, it is important to state that this agency has never defined itself as a Christian organisation. This is in marked contrast to other social work agencies, such as the Church of Scotland social work department which insists on a "live Christian commitment and Church connection" in its advertisements for staff. Family Care therefore provides a useful example of an outwardly secular agency in which, and through which Christian ideas and practices have struggled to be heard.

The process of secularisation

The standard account of the process of secularisation suggests that social and economic change in Western societies has led to a breakdown in authority for organised religion, and an accompanying privatisation and individualisation of religious experience. Religious belief has become something which individuals and families *choose* to get involved in, rather than a kind of social cement for the whole of society - a way of holding people in the same value systems and systems of morality. It is argued that because religion has no meaning outside the private sphere, it has become neutralised, unable to contribute to wider social and political matters. Secular organisations and a myriad of churches and sects have taken the place formerly held by organised religion - we live in a pluralist society. (See Berger, 1969, Brown, 1987, Forrester, 1985.) Wilson (1966) sums this up:-

> The whole significance of the secularisation process is that society does not, in the modern world, derive its values from certain religious preconceptions which are then the basis for social organisation and social action. (Wilson, 1966, pp. 221-233.)

But was Scotland *ever* a society in which Christian values were held by all, and in which the organised Church was viewed as having legitimate control over social and political matters as well as private affairs? Hapgood (1983) argues that there was no halcyon time in the past in Britain when religion was all important, just as there is no secular present where religion plays no part. In reality, the church has always had to struggle to maintain its position and its authority, conventionally by aligning itself with the powerful class and ruling groups in society.

The position is further complicated when we try to define "the church" in Scotland. The Christian church in Scotland is a very broad church, made up of competing groups within and outside the main Protestant tradition. While the established church in Scotland (the Church of Scotland) - like its counterpart the Church of England - played little part in politics in the nineteenth and into the twentieth centuries, the Free Church equivalents and non-conformist churches were deeply committed to social criticism and social change. (Smith, 1987.)

Thomas Chalmers' work in Glasgow in the 1820s and the Christian Socialist movement of the late nineteenth /early twentieth century provide striking examples of different solutions to the struggle within and between Scottish churches to define the place of the church in Scottish society. Chalmers envisaged a "Godly parish" in which all need - welfare, educational, spiritual, pastoral - would be met by a kirk based, local, non-professional system reminiscent of a self sufficient rural parish. Christian socialism on the other hand championed the setting up of baby clinics, sociological investigations, and homes for slum children - institutions which would be run by professionals, instead of needs being met by the church membership. (Brown, 1987.)

From this it is clear that not only is it unlikely that there was some time in the past when the church held absolute control over private and public life, there has never been any simple consensus within the churches about their role and function in society. The church in Scotland today is faced with similar problems. In recent years before the General Assembly of the Church of Scotland meets there has been a public furore about some issue under discussion. In 1994 the spotlight rested on the question of private morality again, principally around church attitudes towards homosexuality and sex outwith marriage. The Panel on Doctrine recommended that faithfulness in relationships mattered more than marriage itself, much to the dismay of many senior Church of Scotland figures.[1] These debates may seem to be of interest only to a marginalised few. But I believe that their significance is much wider than this, and that these controversies shed light on contradictions and continuities which characterise social work enterprise.

In order to examine the Christian discourse within social work I shall use my case study material to explore two main areas. First, I shall examine who is responsible for carrying the Christian discourse forward into social work organisation - that is, "who is speaking?" (Foucault, 1972.) Is it "the Church" (taking into account the difficulties in defining this)? Or is it the clergy or even the lay people themselves? I will then go on to look at the detailed ways in which Christian ideas and practices have been incorporated into social work values and interventions, and ask what significance these have in social work practice today.

Setting the scene: the involvement of the church in the NVA/Guild of Service

When a meeting was called in Edinburgh in the winter of 1911 to discuss the formation of a local branch of the NVA, fifteen clergymen saw it as their business to attend. The meeting was chaired by Rev. Robert J. Drummond, a well known speaker and minister of the United Free Church of Scotland in Lothian Road, Edinburgh. At the end of the meeting, an Executive Committee was formed made up of eight women and nine men, four of whom were ministers. Over the next forty years or so, ministers continued to play an important part in the running of the organisation. Although their numbers gradually reduced, they remained in key posts as committee chairmen, and right up until 1960, the Executive Committee was chaired by a minister, and meetings began and ended with a prayer. Since then, there has been almost no clerical presence on the committees. The one exception was that in 1986, the existing Executive Committee chairman became ordained as a Church of Scotland minister.

So what processes were at work here? Who were these ministers, and why did they disappear from NVA committee work? What does their presence and absence tell us about the religiosity of the social work discourse?

The ministers came from a cross-section of Protestant churches in Edinburgh (Church of Scotland, United Free Church of Scotland, Free Church of Scotland, and Scottish Episcopal Church.[2]) Some were ordinary clergymen concerned about issues of morality as they affected their own districts or parishes. Others were leading churchmen of their day - Moderators of the General Assembly of the Church of Scotland, Principals of New College, Bishops of Edinburgh. Some would undoubtedly have been conservatives, driven by public disquiet about evil conduct and loosening morals in society. Others (like Rev. Drummond and Canon Laurie) were the radicals of their generation - men who highlighted the plight of the urban poor and worked to encourage the church to become actively involved in social action.

The picture of church participation in the NVA (Eastern Division) is however much more complex than my brief introduction suggests. During the early years of the NVA, clergymen did indeed play a major part in the work of the organisation, sitting on committees, chairing public meetings, taking part in deputations, getting involved in practical activities as members of the Men's Committee, including investigating "places of immorality". But the turnover of committee members was high. Some clergymen withdrew their support, disappearing from the scene altogether. Only a very few gave a commitment which was life long.

From the beginning of the Second World War and right through to the 1950s, there was a gradual reduction in *all* men, including ministers, from NVA (now called the Guild of Service) membership. The most active clergymen were those on the Executive Committee, but even here, their actual numbers were small and declining. Between 1938 and 1947, only two out of the fourteen Executive Committee members were ministers; the rest were all women. This figure reduced further to one until 1960 when the last minister died. The Executive Committee remained an all woman committee until 1974.

From this we can see that although ministers did hold positions of authority within the NVA/Guild of Service right up until 1960, their numbers in reality were very small, particularly after the initial burst of enthusiasm which came along with the formation of the Eastern Division. The Scottish churches seem to have been content to leave their ministers to play an individual, informal role in the organisation's work - it was clearly peripheral, rather than central to their concerns, particularly after the "white slave trade" panics of the 1910s had passed over.

The established church in England paralleled this attitude. Although the Archbishop of Canterbury chaired public meetings in 1912 pressing for the Criminal Law (Amendment) Bill to be made law, there was never any formal connection between the NVA and the Church of England. This caused great dissatisfaction amongst the ranks of the NVA, as William Coote, NVA Secretary expressed vehemently:-

> ... the worst difficulty against which we had to contend at that time was the almost sepulchral silence of the Churches. They neither blamed nor praised, but, as in the case of Pilate, washed their hands of all responsibility. (Coote, 1916, p. 25.)

Not only were the actual numbers of clergymen on committees small, it is questionable whether they all saw themselves in a specifically religious role. For a time it was conventional practice to have as many as possible clergy on committees of organisations. They brought respectability and authority to those organisations. Some ministers clearly made committee membership a full time occupation, sitting on many different committees, and attending countless meetings. Brown (1987) suggests that their continued presence in reality masked what he calls a "fundamental secularisation of operations and rationale."

This is extremely important for understanding the shift which took place in this agency. Although a decline in the numbers of clergymen on committees may seem to indicate a decreasing influence of a Christian discourse in the organisation, in fact the Christian discourse within the agency was never held purely in the hands of the clergy. On the contrary, in this organisation it was the women on the committees and in the staff group who held the Christian flame alight, and who devoted their lives to the service of others.

And there is another point here which merits research in its own right. Social work agencies contain within them considerable numbers of men and women who have been, or would have wished to have been clergymen and women themselves - Catholic priests who have chosen to leave the church to get married; women who have been disallowed from expressing their "calling" in full time priesthood.

"Head counts" of ministers therefore tell us little about the religiosity of organisations, or the influence of Christian ideas and values on the activities carried out by the organisation. To find out more about this, we have to turn to the work itself - to the actual practices and strategies adopted by the agency, as described in agency records and interviews with staff, paid and unpaid.

Public and private morality in social work discourse

One of the biggest shifts which we can see taking place in the context of Family Care's history is a move away from Christian explanations and Christian language to describe social problems and social life. There is no better example of this than public and private sexual morality.

Weeks (1981) suggests that the general moral framework of the nineteenth century was unquestionably that of the Christian tradition. This provided the language within which morality (even the morality of non-believers) was articulated, and many of the formal practices which actually regulated sexual behaviour. Laws on incest provide an illustration of this "ecclesiastical regulation". The 1567 Incest Law in Scotland was built on prohibitions which were taken straight from Leviticus.[3]

NVA activity, as I have described in Chapter Two, was wholly centred on Christian ethics, and public and private sexual morality. A concern for prostitution, pornography, homosexuality and obscenity went hand in hand with a re-ordering of the private and public sexual behaviour of men, women and children. The legitimation for this work came from Christian ideology, and the intervention itself was based on Bible teaching on sex and on sin. The NVA message was clear. There was *no* place for sex outwith marriage, and children and young people should be protected from sexual activity until marriage (hence the campaign to raise the age of sexual consent to eighteen and even twenty one years.)

Josephine Butler and other early NVA campaigners believed that they were the carriers of the true Christian message on morality, one which had been forgotten by the Church which was consistently unfaithful to Christ's teaching in its acceptance of the sexual double standard. She re-tells the biblical story of Christ at the temple, where Christ says to his followers who condemn a prostitute, "He that is without sin among you, let him first cast a stone at her." (Butler, 1881.) NVA activists made two demands - first, that women should not be condemned for behaviour excused in men; and second, that *all* men and women should rise above themselves to attain sexual behaviour and morality thought to belong more commonly to women.

Ideas of Christian morality are vividly illustrated in the "rescue work" of the nineteenth and into the twentieth centuries. Although the NVA in Edinburgh did not itself run a rescue home, it referred women constantly to female penitentiaries and Magdalene asylums. (The Glasgow Division did have a residential unit for women.) Rescue work was built on the principle of religious teaching, solitary confinement, and hard labour, usually in the form of laundry work.

Mahood (1990) suggests that the over riding aim of the female penitentiaries was to replace deceit and pride with guilt. Their policy was that each inmate should receive her own Bible as soon as she had learnt to read. The scriptures would reveal the extent of the inmate's sin, defilement and guilt, and she would soon learn to accept herself as a "sinner". The Bible stories also taught a morality centred on self sacrifice and duty:-

> ... through the Christian chain of command which paralleled the Victorian social class hierarchy and which sanctioned female inferiority, self-abnegation and duty, each inmate learned her appropriate gender role and social class position. (Mahood, 1990, p. 83.)

The 1868 Report of the Female Industrial Home at Corstorphine, Edinburgh illustrates this perspective. The secretary/treasurer begins his report:-

> Deliver him from going down to the pit; for I have found a ransom. Job XXXIII. 24.
> Rejoice with me; for I have found my sheep which was lost. Luke XV. 6.
> Dear Friends, The Lord is here calling on us to do two
> things - First, To aid Him in the deliverance of souls that are going down into the bottomless pit, for He has found a ransom. They need not perish. Second, To rejoice with Him over His rescued ones."[4]

The evangelical language used here seems strange and very much from another time. But Bible lessons and the search for codes of morality in the scriptures remained a feature of social work intervention up to the Second World War. When the Organising Secretary began a Sunday afternoon club for girls in domestic service in the 1930s, Bible stories and prayer accompanied tea and conversation. Similarly, a member of staff from the Children's Department in the 1940s described to me encouraging adopters to get down on their knees and pray for the unmarried mother whose child they were about to receive.[5] Her behaviour was considered a bit "over the top" by others with whom she worked, but it was known about and tolerated for many years.[6] Much more recently, children in Edzell Lodge Children's Home were encouraged to say "Grace" before meals and to pray daily, and were marched to Sunday school dressed in their smart "Sunday" clothes right up until the mid 1970s. Of course, we may choose to dismiss the significance of these religious observances, seeing them as meaningless anachronisms, habits left over from a bygone day. Or we may see them as continuing concrete practices, neither accidental nor arbitrary, but in Foucault's words, "regulated by power and knowledge". (Foucault, 1977). They were necessary

46

activities for communicating certain bourgeois values (such as respect for elders and betters, gender roles, place in society) and a particular kind of sexual behaviour and morality.

So how far were these Christian practices forced on clients, and how far did they reflect a continuing Christian legitimacy? Foucault (1977) argues that disciplinary power is not only about regulation in a negative sense - power creates and defines at the same time as it controls. Rewards and privileges go hand in hand with punishments and impositions to create a "normalising judgement" through which it is possible to achieve corrective training. (Foucault, 1977, pp. 176-184.)

NVA records provide evidence of women's often ambivalent experiences of rescue homes. Some young women actively *chose* to go into a training institution which may have offered them an escape from an intolerable home situation, or training for future employment. In the institutions, they were taught to read and to sew, and they were free from unwanted harassment by landlords, parents, or others. There are many examples of letters to NVA workers from grateful women who appear to have wholly identified with the Christian regimes in which they found themselves.[7]

It is impossible seventy years later to be certain about the actual status of these "thank you" letters. Were the women induced to write them as a tactic/practice of the institution? Were the women lying, believing that it would be in their best interests to do so? Had they been in effect brainwashed by the institution so that they were incapable of independent thought? Or could it be that to a certain degree, the Christian principles of the institutions in fact mirrored and corresponded to their own value bases? I believe that the sincerity or otherwise of the letters is less important than the fact that in them we can see the operation of Christian assumptions about sexual morality in practice. Sexual morality is here being created within the Christian discourse.

But there is another dimension here. Foucault argues that wherever there is power, there is resistance - resistance itself has an impact on the application of power. Throughout this agency's history, we can find illustrations of individual and collective resistance, leading to a gradual loosening of public condemnation of both illegitimacy and extra-marital sex.

NVA records are full of accounts of girls running away, leaving institutions, and never being traced again.[8] Women do not always do what the agency wants or expects them to do. Some return to their "former lives" (prostitution); many return to the agency with a second illegitimate pregnancy, in spite of the moral education they received the first time. But it is the struggle to change and finally to close Mother and Baby Homes in Scotland in the late 1960s and early 1970s which provides a concrete example of the workings of resistance in relation to power.

Claremont Park (the Edinburgh Home for Mothers and Infants) was a fairly typical Scottish Mother and Baby Home, and one to which the NVA/Guild of Service was principal referring agent. (Crabbie and Keay, 1985.) It opened in 1924, with the expressed aim of providing pre and post confinement care for "unmarried girls who were expecting their first baby." The Home was run on familiar rescue home lines, with a strict regime which was a mixture of laundry work, housework, prayers in the Home's own Chapel, and of course baby care. A minimum stay of four months was rigidly enforced, because breast feeding was taken for granted, and in order that "the girls might be morally reclaimed":-

> ... through this small Home comes a continual stream of those who instead of being left to slip down into the lowest depths of humanity, are being re-built in character and are given the chance of learning to live, not for themselves alone, but in service to God, their neighbours, to be in fact good citizens.[9]

Claremont Park congratulated itself on its good relationships with its ex-inmates, some of whom returned each year for a reunion tea-party. But during and after the Second World War, resistance to the regime grew. Women who were Guild of Service clients increasingly refused to go to Claremont Park, with its prayers, its enforced breast feeding, and its pressure on women to keep their babies. As casework agencies like the Guild of Service began to champion the rights of children to grow up in two-parent families, campaigning agencies like the Scottish Council for the Unmarried Mother and her Child pressed for the unmarried mothers' views to be taken into account in determining the services which they required.[10] In 1958, the Guild of Service, unable to shift the management at Claremont Park, withdrew its support and the numbers in residence rapidly dwindled to only one in 1960. Claremont Park closed down, and was opened three years later with a new matron, and a new approach. Women now came to the Home largely prior to confinement. Recreation and adoption replaced prayers in the Chapel and unwanted motherhood.

While Mother and Baby Homes like Claremont Park were being forced to make changes in the light of changing social circumstances, so the Guild of Service approach to issues of morality was changing. The shift was witnessed in two main ways. First, the agency no longer saw itself as in the business of trying to change attitudes around public morality and sexual behaviour. When Malcolm Muggeridge campaigned in 1968 against the sale of condoms on the University campus, the Guild of Service stood back and took no part in the debate. At the same time, the agency was developing a casework approach which highlighted new psycho-dynamic concerns, not religious or moral ones. (This theme will be developed fully in Chapter 5.) The professional model which came to prominence focused on individual casework instead of issues of wider public morality.

The new style is seen in the abortion counselling service which operated at the Guild of Service between 1971 and 1973. This agency, working alongside the newly opened Brook Advisory Service, pioneered a service to provide abortion counselling to women with unplanned pregnancies. Its objective was professional, not moral, as it sought to ensure that women had considered fully the alternatives before them, and had examined possible avenues of support. This was not therefore about dissuading women from abortion, or focusing on their guilt or their sin. Rather it was about accepting the reality of abortion, and working to make it as least damaging an experience as possible by drawing on psycho-dynamic insights to enable the woman to understand the origins of her situation and the best outcome. (It was also, significantly, an example of increasing intervention in sexual behaviour, through the development of psy mechanisms of control. See Chapter 5.)

Inevitably some individual social workers found the changed climate difficult to reconcile with their own Christian values. Social workers who worked for the Guild of Service in the late 1960s expressed to me a sense of growing unease as the agency seemed to be moving towards a position of acceptance of extra-marital sexual behaviour. More widely available contraception, abortion and greater tolerance of unmarried motherhood led to some social workers and committee members describing an increasing gap between their own Christian standards of private morality and those seeming to be condoned (and therefore perhaps even encouraged?) by the agency.

Some social workers and committee members disagreed on principle with abortion and contraception believing that it was "too readily available" - that it was better to teach girls to say "no" and to learn to value loving relationships between husband and wife than to "encourage" them to experiment sexually. They therefore disagreed fundamentally with the agency having anything to do with abortion counselling or with the Brook Clinic. (This point of view echoes that expressed by the early vigilance feminists.)

In the 1980s, a new breed of feminist social workers brought a more radical approach to social work and morality. Feminist social workers who believed that women had the right to control their own sexuality took positive steps to support this ideological stance, counselling and befriending women having abortions, providing pregnancy testing kits and contraceptives at the new centre for women and children. But acceptance of these new ideas was never total, and the old, moralistic discourse never disappeared completely. Some committee members continued to hold the view that chastity was better than sexual licence; and that the agency should be very careful in seeming to give backing to women engaged in "immoral" behaviour.[11]

There have been two occasions in recent years when the agency engaged in debate on public morality - both times in connection with the new moral issue of the day, human fertilisation and embryology. Janet Lusk, then Director, was invited to give evidence to the Warnock committee on Human Fertilisation and Embryology which reported in 1984. Then when Kate Priestley was Director, she co-edited a book which was published by Family Care named "Truth and the Child." (Bruce et al, 1988.) Both Directors were keen to raise public awareness and debate on this issue. Their position had little however to do with Christian ideas of morality or Christian ethics. In fact, Kate Priestley encountered opposition from some Christian committee members who felt that the organisation should not be seeming to encourage dubious activities such as surrogacy or donor insemination.[12] Janet and Kate based their opinions firmly on professional social work expertise and practice. Drawing on their knowledge of the experience of adoption, they argued that counselling should be a part of any new procedures, and that openness and honesty should be the norm in the practical procedures.

Individual worth, community and service to others

Christian tradition has not only been influential in defining the context for attitudes and practices in social work concerned with sexual morality. It has in a much broader sense set the tone for social work practice in general, creating the foundations of its value system and providing a framework for its practices.

Social work values and practices are rooted in traditions which are derived from Christian, or Judaeo-Christian discourse. Although expressed today in language which has deliberately foregone its Christian tone, social work is built on assumptions about individual subjectivity, community and service to others which have a strong continuing presence in Christian discourse.

Henderson (1986) suggests that the nub of the Christian faith is that God saved the world by becoming human - "God so loved the world that he gave his only begotten Son." (John 3.16.) As a result, each person is regarded as equal before God. Related to this is the idea of fellowship with others. People have a mutual obligation to one another, because "in as much as you have done it unto one of the least of my brethren, you have done it unto me."

50

(Matthew 31.40.) Christian discourse teaches that in giving service to others, people are serving God. "For even the Son of Man did not come to be served, but to serve." (Mark 10.45.)

Social work and the individual

When the NVA (Eastern Division) began in 1911, work with individuals formed only a part of its work, alongside legislative campaigning, speeches on sex education, investigation of brothels, and street patrolling. As the agency became professionalised however, it was the "individual cases" which began to take up more and more of the agency's time. This mirrors a development which took place throughout the British social work scene, as social work moved away from social action and social reform towards social casework and individual solutions to society's problems. (Seed, 1973.)

The discourse which provided the language for, and the meanings of that shift was not itself a manifestly Christian discourse. Ideas of "client self determination" and "respect for the client" replaced older notions of individual sinfulness and individual responsibility. But the ways in which individual clients were classified, and the methods of intervention used have surprising continuities with older, Christian ideas and practices.

First, we can see similarities in the way in which both discourses name and classify their subjects (that is, their clients.) Both define their clients in terms of a deficit or deficiency in the individual. The NVA never chose to see its subjects as poor, unemployed, economically disadvantaged women who turned to prostitution for financial reasons. Its subjects were instead "victims" - victims of sexual attack or victims of a lack of proper moral training. The clients of the Guild of Service caseworkers were victims too, but in a different sense. As psycho-dynamic ideas began to influence the work in the 1950s and 1960s, women with illegitimate pregnancies were seen as victims of early psychological or emotional damage, or victims of poor socialisation, but victims nonetheless. They were emotionally and psychologically deficient, not morally deficient. (See Donzelot, 1980.) In more recent years, the idea of the victim has continued to pervade agency (and social work) literature. It is much easier to fund raise for single parent families who have been abandoned or for children who are the innocent victims of parental break-up than it is to win public support for single women who have chosen to become mothers.[13]

In his study of punishment, Foucault (1977) identifies continuities not only in the classification of subjects, but also in the actual practices set up to control and regulate subject. He argues that new forms of punishment set out to control the body and "the soul" of the offender:-

51

The expiation that once rained down upon the body must be replaced by a punishment that acts in depth upon the heart, the thoughts, the will, the inclinations." (Foucault, 1977, p. 16.)

There is a clear link between the vigilance era's wish to bring the "miserable sinner" to forgiveness through prayer and confession and the Christian churches' notions of confession and absolution. Newton (1956) describes early probation officers as "missionaries" whose aim was to change behaviour through changing feeling, that is, through "conversion". The new casework approach pioneered in the Guild of Service set out to be different to this. It was to be less judgmental/moralistic/"unprofessional", and influenced by new concepts such as "client self determination". But similarities remained. The power differential still existed between client and counsellor; there was still an expectation that the focus should be on the individual's thoughts and feelings, not the act of wrong doing itself; and the goal remained change in the individual, this time through a process of self examination and insight rather than penitence and absolution. Agency clients complained about being "grilled by social workers". Every detail of their sexual and family history was considered relevant by the new psycho-dynamically oriented social workers.[14]

Social work practice today is still centrally involved in working with individuals - individuals in families, and individuals in communities, but individuals nonetheless. CCETSW's Paper 30 (1989) which lays out minimum standards for social work students at the point of qualification expresses the commitment to the individual as follows:-

Qualifying social workers should have a commitment to
- the value and dignity of individuals;
- the right to respect, privacy and confidentiality;
- the right of individuals and families to choose;
- the strength and skills embodied in local communities;
- the right to protection of those at risk of abuse and exploitation and violence to themselves and others. (CCETSW, 1989, pp. 15-16.)

Social work and the community

Turning to social work's response to the community, we can see throughout this agency's history debates being waged about the place of social work in the community, debates which have in their origins different Christian interpretations of the meaning of charity and community.

The main welfare response to social problems in the nineteenth century

52

came not from the government, but from religious bodies. Philanthropic effort and charity was largely organised and legitimated through Christian religious bodies. (Parry and Parry, 1979, p. 21.) Charity towards the poor and less fortunate in society was held to be a fundamental Christian obligation. How this obligation was to be met, however, has not been so easy to agree on.

Christian ideas of community have been a source of debate within this agency and within social work as a whole. There was a clash between a nineteenth century model of community (that is, the self supporting Godly parish of Thomas Chalmers and his followers) and the state as the community, providing services on its behalf. The President of this agency between the 1960s and 1980s was vehemently opposed to statutory social work on the grounds that it interfered with the community's obligation to look after its own members. The agency's Director, herself a committed Christian, lent more to a Fabian socialist model, seeing a place for both voluntary and statutory social services in a mixed economy of welfare. The difference in perspective can be illustrated in the disagreements between the two women on the principle of receiving children into care. Janet Lusk fought to have the children in Edzell Lodge Children's Home received into care. Such an arrangement meant that not only were the children's boarding costs met, but the local authority was taking what Janet believed to be rightful responsibility for needy children. Lady Learmonth was horrified by this approach. She saw this as "dropping children over the cliff into the hands of the local authority."[15]

More recently, charitable ideas of community have been replaced within social work by a language of rights, advocacy and community self determination which owe much more allegiance to Marxist ideas of structural inequality than to Christian charity. Jordan (1984) suggests that the new awareness of the collective nature of poverty and inequality, and the need for a socialist response, have undermined the older Christian notions of charity and service.

But remnants of older themes remain. This agency (like many social work agencies) still receives gifts at Christmas time to be distributed to needy children; and agency social workers still write "begging letters" each year to the many charitable trusts which give out money and essential items to good causes. As the Conservative government since 1979 has endeavoured to "roll back the frontiers of the welfare state", social workers have found themselves increasingly forced to turn to voluntary agencies for income maintenance and practical support for poor families. Recent community care legislation similarly is built on a model of community involvement which puts the onus back on members of the community (principally women) and not the state, to care for those unable to look after themselves. (Chapter 7 explores this further.)

Social work and service to others

A major shift which has taken place within social work has been a move away from work as Christian vocation to work as profession and career. In interviews with me, early social workers have described their work as a "calling", as a form of missionary vocation from God. The idea of vocation implies that hours worked may be high, and will be related to perceived need rather than payment for a specific job. We can find many examples of this. The paid Organising Secretary in the 1930s and her loyal unpaid supporters staffed church halls at night each autumn for eight years to provide accommodation for sailors from the Home Fleet based at South Queensferry; the Children's Home matron made no distinction between "on" and "off duty" hours. The Organising Secretary believed that her work was carried out on behalf of God - as she said to me, "in all ways acknowledge Him and He shall direct your paths."[16] When the Organising Secretary finally left in 1954, the agency broke with tradition and appointed its first non-practising Christian as Director. What was significant now was not her religious views, but the professional skills and experience she brought with her.

If Christian vocation is less evident in social work today, the idea of service remains. The connection between "service to others" and "service to God" is a persistent theme within social work in this agency. From 1941 until 1978 the agency was known as the Guild of Service - first the Guild of Service for Women (that is, a service *for* women, *by* women) and later simply the Guild of Service.

By interviewing social workers and committee members, I learned that although notions of service may have been overtaken by professional social work and ideas of career, they did not disappear. A great many staff and committee members continued privately to see their work as Christian service. As one committee member said to me, "service is the rent you pay for your space on earth." (This is a "Toc H" motto which was passed on by this committee member's father to her.) And non-Christians too described the impulse to service in the humanitarian tradition. Yelloly (1975) suggests that in the first half of the twentieth century, the concept of charitable service based on duty and paternalistic, class bound relationships gave way to that of social service - service given by individuals on the basis of their shared citizenship.

Service, whether of the charitable or social kind, has had a particularly strong message for women. Miller (1983) points out that serving others is a basic principle around which women's lives are organised. Girls are taught that their main goal is to serve others - first men, and later children - and the result of this upbringing is that women feel compelled "to translate their own motivations into a means of serving others." (pp. 66-67.) Even when women are actually working for other reasons - for financial remuneration, for career development, for social reasons, or for intellectual stimulation - they may reinterpret and rename this work in terms of service.

Gilligan (1987) picks up the question of women's upbringing. She examines the question of sex differences and the differential psychological development of men and women. She concludes that because girls are brought up by those of the same sex, their identification with their carers is much more total than for boys. Girls grow up to define themselves in a context of human relationships, and to judge themselves in terms of their ability to care for others.

It is interesting to speculate that professional social work's rejection of the notion of service in preference for a style centred on contracts and mediation may be connected with the increasing numbers of men taking over positions of power and authority within social work. Notions of service are rarely on the public agenda today in social work practice. A recently published book on social work values makes no mention of Christian values or service. (Horne, 1987.) And yet the evidence of my interviews tells me that service has remained very much alive in the private motivations and rationale of paid and unpaid workers alike.

Adoption practice - changing perspectives

One of the sites which illustrates most clearly the conflict between Christian and secular positions in the agency centres on its adoption practice, and succinctly summed up by the notion that prospective adopters should have a "live church connection".

This stipulation was fundamental to the Organising Secretary from 1929 to 1954. It was the "greatest gift" she could give a child, and her first priority in finding adoptive homes for children. This was not Christianity of a sectarian nature. As she said to me, "it was not about placing a Baptist child with a Baptist family."[17] It was about enabling a child to grow up in a Christian family. Likewise Children's Home matrons were all expected to be devout Christians, so that children would learn "Christian values of service to others".[18]

By the late 1950s, it was found that prospective adopters were approaching sympathetic ministers and asking for references even though they were not regular church attenders. This meant that as a classificatory mechanism, an insistence on a "live church connection" was not working. At the same time, the new stress on individual differences and on approximating a "match" between child and adopters (in terms of physical appearance, intelligence, interests and abilities) meant that a general stipulation such as Christian background was out of favour. The regulation was therefore, after much deliberation, abandoned. Meanwhile, increasingly sophisticated psychological tests and medical predictions of life expectancy were carried out by the new experts in the situation - the Psychiatric and Medical Advisers and the social workers themselves. In other words, the secular discourse won through.[19]

In the early 1980s, adoption again became the focus for Christian versus secular controversy. Staff and committee members were divided on the question of whether a homosexual man should be allowed to adopt a child. The professional assessment of the social work staff supported the application, but committee members over-ruled this assessment. At the core of the controversy, ideas about proper behaviour for men, women and children, about "good role models", and about "correct" sexual behaviour versus "indecent acts" were again played out. The Christian discourse may be seen to have been successful here. But there was another more pragmatic concern. The agency was afraid to go too far ahead of public opinion. Taking such a risky decision might have jeopardised agency funding, and alienated members of the public whose financial support the agency needed.[20]

Today social work agencies endeavour to take a fairly open, perhaps even wary approach to adoptive families' religious beliefs. The Christian discourse has been so discredited within social work that there have been times when a Christian faith has been considered a definite disadvantage. Social workers considering couples for adoption have been critical of those with strongly expressed religious beliefs, fearing that this might indicate an over-rigidity in outlook.[21]

Christian discourse and the social work task today

So how far can we see evidence of the Christian discourse in social work today? What part do Christian ideals and practices play in the formulation of the social work task in the 1990s?

In my own research project, I asked all the respondents whether or not they believed in God, and whether they felt that their personal beliefs had influenced their social work practice in any way. Results displayed a wide spectrum from those who defined themselves as practising Christians, to those who called themselves humanists, agnostics, atheists, feminists and Marxists, or a mixture of some of these. (Family Care has never employed anyone from a different faith, so I was unable to draw any cross-faith comparisons.)

What emerged most clearly was that even in cases of respondents who were not now Christians, almost all had been brought up in strongly Christian families, often with a father who was a priest/minister or a parent who held a position of responsibility in a church, as an elder or vestry member. There was no significant difference between committee members and social workers here. Put simply, almost all of those interviewed could explain their reasons for coming into social work as being related to an early Christian upbringing.

This was a fundamental point of discovery for me, and one which I found very unsettling. I recognised that my own reasons for becoming a social worker were no distance away from those respondents who talked to me about the importance of "service", "working for others" and "giving something back". Brought up in a strongly Christian family, these were familiar childhood themes, from Brownies, Girl Guides, Sunday School, church choir, and from home. Although I had rejected Christianity as an adolescent, I had nevertheless gone into social work, and nineteen years of rationalist, Marxist atheism since then had done nothing to dissolve my strong connections with the women I interviewed. I found myself not only hearing the stories of other women, but also being faced with my own story at the same time.

Accepting that Christian background may be an important factor in the decision to come into social work (at least to come to work in a voluntary organisation like Family Care), what impact does Christian discourse have today on the actual day to day practice of social work? Because the task of social work has been reframed in the language of professional/ bureaucratic/ administrative concerns, it is difficult to see evidence of Christian ideology in mainstream social work practice. What the professionalisation of social work did was to largely outlaw older Christian explanations for, and solutions to social problems. (See Chapter 4.) A recent study by Ashford and Timms (1990) reinforces this analysis. They found in their study of two statutory and four voluntary agencies carrying out family placement work that there were no differences in actual practice between different agencies, even though there were significant differences between agencies in terms of the religious beliefs expressed by their social workers. They conclude that first and foremost, family placement is a "professionally governed enterprise."

Christians in social work have not however been content to stand back from the ideological battleground which is the social work task. The Social Workers' Christian Fellowship was founded in 1964 with the specific aims of promoting the Christian discourse within social work. The Fellowship's declared objective is not to evangelise with social work clients. Instead, the stress is on supporting Christian social workers and pressing the adoption of Christian principles within professional social work practice.

The aims of the Social Workers' Christian Fellowship are as follows:-

To increase the personal faith in Jesus Christ of those working in the field of social welfare and to promote the acceptance of Biblical ethical teaching;

To clarify the thinking of its members on professional matters in the light of Biblical principles, and to encourage them to make these views heard at every professional level;

To encourage Christians coming into social work to integrate their personal beliefs with their professional practice.

Specific projects have been set up as examples of Christian social work programmes, for example, the Southdown Community Project in Easterhouse, Glasgow, sponsored by the Church of England Children's Society, and led by Bob Holman. He outlines the necessary features in a Christian approach to social work. These are serving others (being ready to listen, being available, doing practical, useful tasks for others); making a commitment to local involvement as a means of promoting oneness and togetherness; working co-operatively without hierarchical structures and job demarcation. (Holman, 1986)

Interestingly, the part of Family Care's work which most resembles Bob Holman's picture of a Christian project is No. 20, Family Care's centre for women and children in Muirhouse. The underlying principles which determine No. 20's practice are not Christian ones, but feminist ones. But both projects involve a rejection of some of the principle tenets of professional social work - professional distance, professional expertise, and professional power. (The links between feminism and Christianity are explored by Storkey, 1985.)

Social work in the voluntary sector in Scotland today remains very much in the hands of Christian churches and organisations, even when these agencies choose to play down their Christian connections. It is the Church of Scotland, the Catholic Church, the Scottish Episcopal church and the Salvation Army which carries out most of the work with destitute and homeless people in Scotland today, as well as substantial provision for the elderly and projects which work with "outcast" groups such as prostitutes, drug users and alcoholics. In some of these settings, pockets of missionary zeal remain, for example, the spiritual healing which is a constituent part of an Edinburgh alcohol rehabilitation project.

Summary

I believe that Christian discourse (itself in a constant process of change and negotiation) has played an important part in shaping and defining the terms of reference of the social work task. Certainly, Family Care has moved a long way from the days when social workers prayed with their clients, or described the agency's good fortunes in terms of miracles from God.[22] But there is a sense in which a change in the language of discourse did not necessarily imply a change in the discourse itself. The language may have changed, but the older themes, about sexual morality and the place of women, about the individual, community and service, remained and became incorporated (alongside other socialist, psycho-dynamic, and pluralist notions) into the melting pot of ideas and practices which we today call social work. By looking at social work today, we can see some of the same battles re-enacted, battles about how welfare should be best provided; about the continuing usefulness of categories such as "moral danger"; about public and private morality.

Since Christian discourse is inevitably changing and being reformed at the same time as social work is, a "catch-all" concept such as secularisation must be treated with caution. Nevertheless, there has indeed been a secularising of the social work task, even within this agency, built as it was on strongly Christian foundations. The Christian perspective was not lost completely. It continued to exist in the personal beliefs and motivations of individual social workers and committee members, but disappeared from the formal organisation and professional activities, except at moments of celebration. (For example, Services of Thanksgiving were held to mark the 60th and 80th Birthdays of the agency.) Christian ideas and practices were effectively silenced by the new professional/ psycho-dynamic discourse and went underground; in other words, they were "privatised."

This is not to claim that Christian ideas and practices have been silenced for ever. I believe that the Christian discourse remains implicit in the knowledge base and practices particularly of voluntary social work agencies, and may currently be undergoing something of a revival in social work, with a new generation of Christian social workers prepared to argue their case and work to see that Christian insights and ideas remain on the social work agenda.

I leave the last words in this chapter to Michel Foucault (1972):-

To say that one discursive formation is substituted for another is not to say that a whole world of absolutely new objects, enunciations, concepts, and theoretical choices emerges fully armed and fully organised in a text that will place that world once and for all; it is to say that a general transformation of relations has occurred, but that it does not necessarily alter all the elements... (Foucault, 1972, p. 173.)

Notes

1. Iain Torrance, "Outsider" column, *Herald*, 18-05-94.
2. Of these 15 clergymen, 4 were Church of Scotland ministers; 5 United Free Church of Scotland ministers; 2 Scottish Episcopal Church ministers; 1 Free Church of Scotland minister; and I have been unable to trace the religious affiliation of the remaining 3 - possibly Methodist, Congregationalist or Pentecostal. There was no representation from the Roman Catholic or Jewish Church.
3. England and Wales did not make incest a criminal offence until 1908, reflecting a new eugenic concern about blood relations.
4. J.H. Maitland, Secretary/Treasurer, in 1868 Report of Female Industrial Home at Corstorphine.
5. Interview, 12-11-89.
6. Interview with Janet Lusk, 18-05-90.
7. Case records, 1910s and 1920s.
8. Case records, 1910s and 1920s.
9. Claremont Park Annual Report, 1941.
10. The Scottish Council for the Unmarried Mother and her Child began an Occupancy Service in 1967, with the expressed intention of closing Mother and Baby units down. It was felt that only hard facts would convince the management committees of these Homes that there was no future for Mother and Baby Homes as presently managed. (Interview, 18-02-91.)
11. Interview, 27-05-91.
12. Policy Committee minutes, 1987.
13. Interview, 01-02-91.
14. Scottish Council for the Unmarried Mother and her Child Conference Papers, 1971.
15. Interview, 27-01-94.
16. Interview, 17-07-90.
17. Interview, 17-07-90.
18. Interview, 17-07-90.

Continued

19. Interview with Janet Lusk, 18-05-90.
20. Interview with Janet Lusk, 18-05-90.
21. Interview, 13-04-91.
22. Annual Report, 1954.

4 The professionalisation of social work

Introduction

The history of British social work is the history of a professionalising occupation. (Parry and Parry, 1979, p. 26). Social work has fought to achieve and to maintain a measure of professional control and organisational unity. The battle has taken place both within and outwith the body of social workers, as those inside and out have sought to define the functions and boundaries of the social work task.

As the task of social work has expanded, so it has increasingly become a statutory activity performed under the auspices and management of the state. Two specific and inter related trends are apparent here. Occupational growth has gone hand in hand with a diminution of professional independence. Social work has become an activity more and more regulated by legislation and by local authority codes of practice. At the same time, agencies which had been at the centre stage of the professionalising process - forward thinking, highly specialised voluntary organisations like this one and teaching institutions - have gradually seen their power and control diminished, as large scale welfare bureaucracies increasingly set the agenda for the future of social work policy and practice.

The history of Family Care is the history of one branch of social work's attempts to professionalise itself and to professionalise social work as a whole. It is also the story of its failure in this larger goal, as it became more and more side-lined in both its activities and its influence. (This will be explored more fully in Chapter Seven.)

Definitions - the nature of a profession

The question of what constitutes a profession has received much academic attention. Some sociologists have adopted an absolute approach which defines occupations as professional or non-professional, depending on how they match up to the traditional professions of law, medicine and the ministry. (Flexner, 1915; Greenwood, 1957; Wilkenski, 1964.) Other sociologists prefer a more relative approach, placing different occupations at various points along a continuum from professional to non-professional. (Carr-Saunders, 1965; Etzioni, 1966; Toren, 1972.)

Which ever is the case, all these attempts rely on a scheme of categorisation of the essential ingredients which must be present for an occupation to be held to be professional. Typically these include specialist knowledge and skills, a recognised body of theory, the existence of a professional association, restrictions on entry and the necessity of a period of training. There is disagreement about the relative weight to be given to each of these characteristics, and disagreement too about where different occupations should be placed on the occupational scale. Unsurprisingly, social work has been variously described as professional, semi-professional and non-professional; a new, aspiring, emergent, and personal service profession.

Debate over the nature of a profession highlights the reality that the terms "profession" and "professional" are not value free and neutral, but on the contrary, carry with them special privileges, status and power. "Professional" work is viewed as worthy of merit and carries with it higher social standing. "Unprofessional", or "non-professional" work is somehow sub-standard, inferior, and carried out by people of less ability or lower social class. (Becker, 1962.) Illich (1977) takes up this theme. He argues that professional power is a specialised form of the privilege to prescribe:-

> ... it is the power of prescription that gives control within the industrial state. Professionals tell you what you need and claim the power to prescribe. (Illich, 1977, p. 17.)

Foucault makes a similar observation. He argues that knowledge is not the sum of what is actually or even thought to be true. On the contrary, it is "the whole set of practices, singularities and deviations of which one could speak in a discourse." (Foucault, 1982, p. 182.) My analysis of professionalisation sets out to be as wide ranging and inclusive as this.

The process of professionalisation

There have been many attempts to delineate the process of professionalisation - that is, to explain the stages of its development. Wilenski (1964) outlines five main stages in the professionalisation process of occupations in the United States.

1   A new occupational group emerges, engaged in full time, non manual work on a particular set of problems;
2   Training and selection procedures are set up;
3   A professional association is formed;
4   The occupation agitates for public support;
5   A code of ethics is elaborated. (Wilenski, 1964, pp. 113-115.)

Wilenski has been criticised for presenting a model which is historically and culturally specific. Elliott (1972) reworks his model, envisaging four stages in the professionalisation of social work, arguing that each may lead to changes not only in the formal structure of the occupation, but also in the occupation's means and goals.

Fundamental to the idea of a professionalisation process is the acceptance that something definable as a "profession" exists, and that its progress can be charted irrespective of the context in which it occurs. But the professionalisation of social work cannot be understood outwith the historical and political context. It did not happen automatically or even incrementally. It was fought for and by a group of people who had vested interests in upgrading their status in society, a group largely made up in the early stages of middle class women. In the case study of Family Care, the leadership and drive in the organisation came almost totally from middle class women, from its beginnings to the present day, as directors, committee members, and staff. (See Chapter Six.) In their push to professionalise their work, they sought to build a knowledge base for social work, and to achieve the status and recognition in their occupational lives that they already expected to receive in their private lives. The means to achieving this end was to make a distinction between themselves and all others involved in social work, principally untrained welfare workers and ex-Poor Law personnel, but also volunteers, church visitors and carers.

Class and gender in the professionalisation of social work

Johnson (1972) proposes that an analysis of the professions must take into account macro issues such as the social division of labour and power, instead of the minutiae of the culturally and historically specific micro analyses which have been given so much attention. From this perspective, the professionalisation of social work must be understood as part of the process of the rise to power of an urban middle class at the end of the nineteenth and beginning of the twentieth centuries. More explicitly, it occurred in the context of the demands of women for an increased role in the public domain, and a greater recognition of the value of their work.

Parry and Parry (1979) examine the formation of women's occupations in the nineteenth century, occupations such as teaching, nursing and almoning (medical social work), all of which were committed to professional training and some degree of self management, and which modelled themselves on the values of professionalism which they shared with the men of their social class. Witz (1990) takes this analysis one step further. She points out that the generic notion "profession" is inevitably a gendered notion because "it takes what are the successful projects of class privileged male actors at a particular point in history and in particular societies to be the paradigmatic case of profession." (p. 675.) She concludes that professionalisation can only be understood as a strategy of occupational closure, a series of tactics to keep others out, and must be explored in the context of the structural and historical parameters of patriarchal capitalism.

This reflects earlier work by Johnson (1977). Here he argues that the kind of occupational control or professionalism which an occupation achieves is related to the requirements of capital. In terms of social work, then, what is most significant about its professional status is the increasing absorption of social work activity into the welfare state. It is the state which defines need and the manner in which it shall be met, and which guarantees clients for the social worker:-

> The client of the probation officer (social worker) is then *produced* and guaranteed by the workings of the system of justice. (Johnson, 1977, p. 108.)

The clients of a voluntary organisation might not be thought to have such a symbiotic relationship with the state. Voluntary social work agencies have always prided themselves on their ability to act independently and to initiate unhampered by state control. However, one of features of the professionalisation process has been an increasing convergence between different social work activities. Voluntary and statutory social work are both governed by a host of statutes and legislation which define the nature of the work and how it should be carried out. At the same time, the state (local and central government) has become a major funder of voluntary enterprise. (See Chapter Seven.)

Donzelot (1980) sets the process of professionalisation in the context of the emergence during the nineteenth century of a new "space of knowledge" which he calls the realm of "the social." He proposes that a transition has taken place from a government *of* families to a government *through* the family; a shift from coercive and punishment oriented models of social control to a system of "policing" of families which relies on the new "psy" professions to be its executives - doctors, psychiatrists, psychologists, health visitors, and of course, social workers. The policing of families can be evidenced in a host of new regulations and practices concerning the care of children - in the establishment of ante natal and postnatal care; of free school meals and school medical inspections; of educational and health service clinics; of health visiting and social work services; of rules governing a range of subjects including adoption, boarding out of children, and residential homes for children. This is not policing in a narrow, repressive sense, or relating only to the requirements of capital. Instead it is a way of encompassing all the practices which together unite to control and regulate our lives. (Donzelot is here developing Foucault's analysis of the productive aspects of power. See Foucault, 1977.)

In summary, whether or not we believe that social work merits the status of a profession, and whatever we accept as the essential stages in professionalisation, the social work task has changed profoundly over the period of Family Care's life, and these changes have been part of a deliberate strategy engaged by social workers to upgrade their authority and their position in the professional sphere, and to improve their social work practice. Drawing on Foucault's methodology, the crucial questions are not what is a profession?, or what is the process of professionalisation? We should ask rather, why did the change happen now?; who is in charge of the new discourse?; how is it that this speaker and this discourse "derives its legitimate source and point of application - its specific objects and instruments of verification?" (Foucault, 1972, p. 51.) The professionalisation of social work did not happen in an easy, unproblematic way. There were struggles inside and outside social work, and the social work task today reflects the nature of the winners and the losers in this struggle, as well as the compromises made along the way.

The NVA, professionalism and social work

When this agency began as the NVA (Eastern Division) in 1911, and more particularly when its parent-organisation began in 1885, it did not call itself a social work agency. Something which might be regarded as social work took place in the support work carried out with stranded and vulnerable young women. But the primary focus in the agency's work was campaigning - campaigning for a transformation in sexual relations between men, women and children. NVA staff and committee members in Edinburgh in the early days of the organisation displayed a marked ambivalence to their involvement in "social work". This was evident in the publications to which they subscribed (vigilance, not social work magazines), and the conferences to which they attended (on white slavery, not social service). But as the work of the agency gradually came to be more and more taken up with the "mother and baby cases", so this emphasis shifted, and the social work role came to achieve more prominence.

This raises a much wider question - what was social work at the beginning of the twentieth century? The answer is that social work was anything and everything, from the casework of the Charity Organisation Society, to the social reform based settlement movement, to the institutional and non-institutional care provided by a large number of Poor Law and philanthropic organisations. Most social work was provided by voluntary agencies. We can see the beginnings of statutory intervention around this time, but the majority of social care was still in the hands of voluntary organisations, and carried out, on the whole, by middle class women and some men. (See Prochaska, 1980 and Jordan, 1984, and Chapter Seven.)

What we see happening in the first half of the twentieth century is the narrowing of the task of social work. Social work gave up its claim to be a social movement and chose to concentrate instead on social casework with individuals and families. The decline of the vigilance cause can be seen as part of this general shift away from changing society to changing individuals. Seed (1973) asserts that social work as a social movement after the Second World War was "a pale shadow of the old movement at the end of the nineteenth century, with its vast claim then to the formula for social advance." He concludes that the hopes of those who wished to see a better society turned to political movements. (p.45.)

While the NVA (Eastern Division) may have had doubts in the early stages about its social work remit, it had no such doubts about its professionalism. From the outset it saw itself as a professional organisation. Two major factors distinguished it as a professional agency. First, the staff were expected to be trained, and second, the membership of committees was of a high calibre.

In common with the NVA nationally, local NVA staff were expected to have a relevant training in vigilance or rescue work. The first outdoor worker appointed by the NVA (Eastern Division) in 1912 was Miss Taylor, trained at St Agnes House in London.[1] The work which she was trained in was vigilance or "rescue" work, bearing more similarities to police work than social work. Training included practical, on the spot guidance about how to approach people on the streets, how to avoid getting assaulted, what religious/Biblical texts to draw on in working with cases. There was also some elementary social science, and a firm grounding in Christian ethics and ideology. Because the work centred on questions of morality, this was believed to be the central focus in training. (For a good account of this training, see Cobbold, 1935.)

While employees were expected to be trained, agency leadership and direction came from committee members. There was a clear demarcation of roles between voluntary committee members who made policy decisions and attended conferences, and paid employees who were instructed in their duties. Employees were known as "outdoor workers" - they literally carried out the work on the streets, outside the institutions. There are strong parallels here with the management of other voluntary agencies, for example the Charity Organisation Society. The COS was founded and run by middle and upper class beneficiaries, while paid workers were drawn from the "superior sort" of working men. (Parry and Parry, 1979, p. 27.) The NVA drew in its early years on "superior working women", since work with women and children was regarded as women's work.

All policy matters and decision making about staffing, structure, fund-raising and use of resources in the NVA was the responsibility of the Executive Committee which met monthly, and the much larger General Committee which met less frequently but had ultimate responsibility for major decisions. The men and women who were on both committees, and sometimes also on the Ladies Committee (which oversaw the work with young women), played a significant role in the running of the organisation. They took part in deputations, attended conferences, drafted letters and resolutions on vigilance matters, local and national. Committee members also played a limited part in the outdoor work, and helped in the office when funds were scarce. At other times, special groupings were formed to tackle specific pieces of work. For example, a Men's Committee was formed in 1912 to investigate allegations of immoral behaviour (in this case, male prostitution) taking place at the top of Calton Hill in the centre of Edinburgh in the hours of darkness. (This was considered to be "improper" work for the outdoor worker.)

The NVA's approach to professionalism is evident in its support for paid police women. During the First World War, voluntary "women patrols" operated on the streets and in the stations, supported by, and strengthening the work of the NVA outdoor workers. While agreeing to work alongside the untrained women patrols because of the exigencies of war, the NVA locally and nationally campaigned for a professional women's police presence, and for the establishment of permanent paid police women. In Edinburgh the NVA paid the wages of two "women police" (as they were then called) for ten months in 1919. They hoped that by proving the usefulness of women police in practice, the local council would be persuaded to accept the need for them, and make them part of the police establishment. During World War Two, the Executive committee argued against the re-establishment of voluntary women patrols in Edinburgh, on the grounds that they were "non trained."[2]

The distinction being made here is not between those who are paid and unpaid, but between those who have received the necessary training and those who have not. There were times in the NVA's history when it was unable to pay its staff, and workers had to be laid off. In 1915 when the agency was critically short of cash, a woman known to a committee member offered to work in a newly designated position of organising secretary without pay for six months, receiving instead free board and lodgings and domestic help. Payment for work was not therefore a crucial factor in determining an agency's professional status. This illustrates a common phenomenon in social work at that time. Walton (1975) suggests that there was no devaluing of voluntary work as against paid, "professional" work, and that this was to come later. (p. 147.)

Another example of the agency defining its professional boundaries is seen in 1923. When the Council of Social Service invited the NVA and other voluntary bodies to join them on a case committee to discuss the management of "more permanent rescue cases", the NVA declined.[3] They were concerned about confidentiality, and stated that this kind of work should only be undertaken by trained rescue workers. (Such sentiments would be very familiar to "professional" social workers today.)

The professionalisation of social work

A simple way of analysing the professionalisation of social work in Family Care is to examine the process chronologically in terms of the three stages. In the first stage, vigilance campaigning and street patrolling gradually gave way to what can be defined as "moral welfare", and children increasingly became a major focus of concern. This stage roughly follows the period when Miss Kay Stewart was Organising Director, from 1929 to 1954. The second stage marks the appearance of a very different kind of social work in the agency, as Dr Alexina McWhinnie (Director, 1957 to 1962) set out to "professionalise the service". Stage three represents another shift. While social work continued to consolidate its professional status through professional associations and the emergence of generic social work, professional social work was under attack from new radical ideas which challenged its hegemony, and from a series of child abuse tragedies which questioned social work's ability to live up to its promises and its expectations. This period coincides with the Directorship of Miss Janet Lusk, from 1962 to 1984.

To examine the transformation according to the periods of leadership of the Directors does not, of course, imply that I believe that all the changes were directly attributable to these three figures. On the contrary, they were all a part of, and illustrative of the continuum of controversy and debate around professionalisation, that is, they were a part of the discourse around professionalisation. Foucault (1972) reminds us that certain individuals give particular perspectives a sharp formulation at particular points in time - they gather together threads already available in the "space of knowledge". (pp. 193-194.) The new "space of knowledge" which was moulding professional social work was a whole melting-pot of theoretical concepts, legislation and changing attitudes towards the role of the state in intervening in people's lives.

Stage one: moral welfare replaces vigilance and policing, 1929-1954

During Miss Stewart's long association with Family Care (at first called the NVA, then after 1941, the Guild of Service for Women) we can identify a gradual shift away from old vigilance concerns and issues towards a reformulation of the work as social casework. At the same time, there was a renegotiation of the management of the work, as members of staff sought to have control of the professional work of the agency for the first time. This does not imply that everything shifted all at once (it did not) or that there was no continuity (which there clearly was.) Miss Stewart acted as a bridge between the old and the new - between the old, moralistic discourses and the new professional casework ideas; between powerful committee members and new professionally trained caseworkers.

Miss Kay Stewart's appointment to the post of Organising Secretary at the NVA in 1929 marked a turning point in the history of the agency. Although her father had been a missionary, Miss Stewart had not been trained in rescue work, and instead was a graduate of the new Social Studies course at Edinburgh University. This means that although her personal values were steeped in Christian tradition, her training was much broader than traditional

70

rescue work training. She had studied everything from political economy to social history and social administration, and had a different concept of poverty, need, and the legitimate role of the helping organisations.

New projects begun by Miss Stewart evidence this distinction. Young women were still taken to and from institutions and places of work, but Miss Stewart broadened the intervention far beyond the limitations of conventional vigilance work. She took on whole new areas of work, including girls' clubs and work with prisoners' families, marital counselling, and support for a small number of elderly women who had been evicted from live-in domestic positions. She also provided accommodation for sailors from the Home Fleet stationed in South Queensferry in the years up to the Second World War. In 1933 she wrote, "No matter what the trouble, we are willing to lend a hand."[4] The Objects of the agency changed in 1930 to allow for this shift in direction away from protection in terms of white slavery towards a more open, all encompassing protection for women and girls.[5]

While the NVA concentrated its focus of attention on what came to be called moral welfare, social work itself was enlarging across many fronts. In 1947 Younghusband wrote a report on the employment and training of social workers in which she laid down the existing parameters and functions of social work. Included in the forms of social work were almoning, child care, church work, colonial service welfare, community centre and settlement work, community organisation, family casework, information and advice services, moral welfare, personnel management, the physically and mentally handicapped, probation and other court work, psychiatric social work, youth leadership, and social workers in the civil service. She herself admitted:- "The net result is to demonstrate the hopeless and unprofitable task of determining the frontiers of social work." (p. 104.)

But social work activities did not simply reflect agency priorities and preferences. Social changes transformed the social work of this and other agencies in the period during and between the two World Wars. The volume and nature of NVA cases changed dramatically in the period up to the beginning of the Second World War. The total number of cases more than doubled between 1930 and 1940, and there was an ever increasing percentage of "mother and baby cases". These cases which had been seen as "outwith the remit of this agency " in 1919 became one third of the cases by 1939, and this figure continued to rise throughout the Second World War. Quite simply, there were more illegitimate pregnancies, and what was in the beginning a small part of the agency's work became the most significant part. (Again, the agency's Objects changed to take account of this shift.)[6]

The mother and baby cases demanded a great deal of work, both before and after the baby's birth. The task of the social worker (called a "caseworker"

71

by the early 1940s) was to explore with the pregnant woman and her family what needed to happen for her to keep the baby. (This was quite unlike the open ended, self determining casework which was to become the proper, "professional" style in the future.)[7] Arrangements had to be made for the confinement, and for the after-care, which usually meant domestic service with or without the baby, and/or a private fostering placement for the baby. Putative fathers were contacted with regard to paying a contribution for maintenance of the child. (The letter sent to the father was called affectionately by staff "the snorter".)[8] Adoptions were rare, since it was generally believed that women would be less likely to have a second illegitimate child if they were encouraged to care for their first one. Miss Stewart expressed this clearly:-

> There is no character-building experience to be derived by a young girl who has the inconvenient consequences of her behaviour removed.[9]

The opening of a children's home in 1947 must be seen in the context of both changes in the client group and new ideas on child development and children's needs. Edzell Lodge was opened primarily as a resource for unmarried mothers. As numbers of births to unmarried parents rose, (see Figure 1), so numbers of foster parents declined rapidly during the Second World War, and there was a crisis of placement opportunities for illegitimate children. The impetus to open a Home came from the need to find suitable accommodation for illegitimate children. The regime of the Home, once opened, reflected the new psychological ideas and practices.

Changes in the staff and in the client group were mirrored by changes in the role of the committees. Very broadly, with Miss Stewart's appointment in 1929 we see responsibility for initiative and direction in the agency passing from the committee to the Organising Secretary. The worker was no longer simply an employee who did the bidding of a powerful and controlling committee. The committee was still there, and still hearing reports of her work. But it is clear from agency records that as the agency moved away from general campaigning work into individual casework, so committee members felt less qualified to be involved in the management of the work. Soon it was Kay Stewart who was generating the ideas, and the committee were delighted to support her in her initiatives.[10]

But as I have indicated already, professionalisation is not always accompanied by consensus and agreement. On the contrary, it is also the site of contestation and disagreement, as individuals struggle to maintain power, and as competing discourses fight to be heard and to gain prominence. In this agency, the conflicts inherent in professionalisation are encapsulated in

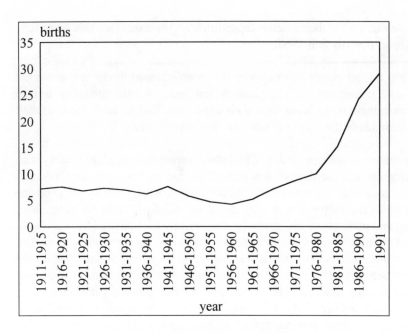

Source: Registrar General for Scotland, Annual Report, 1991, General Register Office, Edinburgh, p. 19.

Figure 1 Births to unmarried parents per 100 live births, Scotland, 1911-1991

the breakdown of the relationship between Miss Stewart and Lady Learmonth, the most powerful committee member over a long period, and herself a trained medical social worker from the United States.

Charlotte Learmonth joined the Executive Committee in 1944. Unable to work in a paid capacity herself (because of her position as a professor's wife) she offered her services on a voluntary basis to the Guild of Service for Women. Her choice of this agency was solely on the grounds that this was the only agency in Edinburgh with a professionally qualified social worker at the helm.[11] Mrs Learmonth spent her first year getting to know the work of the agency by working alongside Miss Stewart as an unpaid caseworker. Then in 1944 she agreed to accept nomination to the Executive Committee, where she set about up-grading and professionalising the committees and the agency's work.

She described the Executive Committee in 1944 as "an over-balanced committee, only supporting one aspect of the work - the financial".[12] Her self appointed task was therefore to recruit new committee members who would give a better level of support to the professional work of the agency -

"people chosen for their known capabilities". She expressed this more fully in a report published in 1965:-

> Far deeper possibilities existed for an enlightened group of women not only to support the organisation, but under the leadership of trained caseworkers, to learn from their experience and so carry back to their community the leaven of new and progressive ideas.[13]

Committee members under Charlotte Learmonth's tutelage were soon carrying out diverse duties on behalf of the agency - visiting the Children's Homes to advise on matters of "housewifely concerns"[14]; befriending the children in the Homes; reviewing cases for adoption or foster care; fund-raising and publicity work. Lady Learmonth saw the potential for a group of unpaid women, most of whom were doctors' wives, to carry out a supportive role to the professional staff at the same time as acting as monitors of the service delivery. Her approach caused more than a little friction within the agency, leading to some older committee members leaving, (described to me as "the old ladies with hats".)[15] Lady Learmonth was also instrumental in the setting up of new inter-agency child care committees in Edinburgh, for example, the Edinburgh Children's Welfare Group, and the Edinburgh Children's Homes Organisation.

Lady Learmonth's impact on the actual social work practice of the agency is more difficult to quantify. Agency records give the impression that all the innovation in service provision was coming from Miss Stewart, who wrote the Annual Reports, carried out much of the work, and trained the assistant caseworkers. But interviews which I have conducted suggest that Lady Learmonth was increasingly influential in decision making about policy and practice in terms of child care, and that Miss Stewart felt increasingly isolated. Eventually, Miss Stewart resigned in 1954, unable to reconcile herself to a specific difference of opinion over a child in care.[16] The agency then waited for three years until a person of "high enough calibre" could be appointed in her place.

The breakdown between Miss Stewart and Lady Learmonth reflects the struggle in the agency between moral welfare and casework as the legitimate object and strategy. Moral welfare was being eroded throughout the social work world - medical social workers, probation officers, children's officers, marriage guidance workers, youth workers, religious education teachers were all taking over bits of what had been moral welfare's responsibility. The moral welfare course which Miss Stewart had fought to establish in Edinburgh collapsed after only one year in 1948 because of insufficient numbers of applicants, and increasingly, the moralistic discourse was coming under attack from the new professional social work discourses, from medical social work, psychiatric social work and later child care.

Stage two: streamlining the service, 1957-1962

When Dr McWhinnie began as Director in 1957, she came to an agency which she already knew. She had worked for Miss Stewart for two years as an assistant caseworker before going on to do a Ph.D. on experiences of adoption. (McWhinnie, 1967.) She came to the agency with an already worked out plan for professionalising the service, and spent the next five years working to put her ideas into practice. The shift in policy and practice post 1957 was therefore neither accidental nor incremental. Rather, it can understood as a deliberate attempt to re-shape agency policy and practice to fit perceived standards of professional organisation and professional systems, mirroring medical models of consultation and aetiology and business models of structure and bureaucracy, and at the same time building on knowledge of good practice gained from her own and from current North American research findings.

Dr McWhinnie introduced changes at management, administrative and practice levels, all aimed at what she saw as upgrading and "professionalising" the service. The Director became responsible for the professional development of the agency, in terms of policy development and improvements in actual casework practice. She held a caseload of adoptive couples, and instituted a system of regular, detailed supervision of the work of the other caseworkers. (This model, adapted from North American social work practice, was being adopted in predominantly psychiatric social work settings in Britain.) Because she was fully occupied with "professional" concerns, a new post of agency Secretary/Treasurer was created to take charge of all financial and administrative matters.

In order to achieve these changes, the organisation needed to be on a firmer financial footing. This was achieved by the opening in 1956 of the first Thrift Shop in Scotland - another North American idea, this time introduced by Lady Learmonth and her friends. The agency also benefited greatly from a cash injection after Springwell House closed in 1954. (This had in former years been Edinburgh's Magdalene Asylum.)

The role of the committees had to change too. Although the Executive and General Committees continued to meet, increasingly the professional decision making of the agency took place in other arenas, where paid caseworkers played a major role. The large committees concentrated instead on practical matters such as staffing and publicity.

Dr McWhinnie gathered around herself a number of experts whom she

75

could call on - paediatricians, child psychiatrists, university teachers, lawyers, prominent medics. Some took part in new groupings. An Advisory Council was set up in 1955, and the following year Adoption and Child Care committees began, where experts worked alongside lay committee members to advise and assist in the process of ratifying caseworkers' professional recommendations on matters such as selecting couples for adoption, and the placement of babies for adoption.

Some professionals gave their input in other ways. They examined babies, advised on points of law, and carried out assessments of prospective adopters' psychiatric history and potential life expectancy. The caseworker's task was to draw together the professional assessments of others and to make a recommendation based on the sum total of these and of her own findings. The role of the committees was to ratify the professional recommendations and to maintain the quality of service.

Through all these changes, significantly, Dr McWhinnie had the support of Lady Learmonth who was delighted with the general shift towards more professional standards.[17] Some committee members were less enthusiastic. They found the new style committees too high powered and moved instead to giving service by working in the newly opened Thrift Shop. But committee members were not the only casualties. Three of the four existing members of staff who had worked prior to Dr McWhinnie's arrival left within a year, finding the changes incompatible with their approach to the work.[18] One new appointment was that of Miss Janet Lusk, fresh from the new Child Care course at Birmingham University, and soon to be appointed Director herself in 1962.

Alongside the changes in management in the agency we can see a shift in the agency's clients. The "general casework" help which had been given to a broad range of clients perceived to be at risk was narrowed to become a specialist service targeted at a limited client group made up of predominantly single parents and their children.[19] This "streamlining of the service", as Dr McWhinnie referred to it in the 1958 Annual Report, meant that cases seen as inappropriate to the agency were now referred on elsewhere, for example, elderly women and travellers were passed on to other agencies such as Old People's Welfare and YWCA. With a more narrowly defined area of work, and with extra social work and secretarial staff employed to carry out the work, the agency was free to develop its policy and procedures in what was to become the agency's field of excellence, that is, in adoption practice. This change must, in turn, be set in the context of the growing statutory services and the need for voluntary agencies to clearly define their pitch.

Changes in adoption practice illustrate the desire within social work to make its systems more "scientific" and more professional, by building a social work practice which was based on knowledge and skill, not intuition and common sense experience. The source of this new knowledge and practice was literature and research by psychologists, psychiatrists and other social scientists, with the Child Welfare League of America playing a significant role in disseminating new ideas. Dr McWhinnie's own research contributed to the available knowledge about adoption. (McWhinnie, 1967.)

Dr McWhinnie had interviewed fifty eight adopted adults to find out how adoption had affected them in their lives. From this she was able to construct a picture of what had been helpful/important, unhelpful/unimportant in their experience of adoption, and so make an analysis of what would be good adoption practice in the future. Her research led her to seek ways of "reducing the risks" of adoption - not predicting the future as such, but reducing the likelihood of future problems.[20] This was to be achieved by a much more thorough approach to assessment in adoption - assessment of the baby, the adopters and the birth (biological) parents of the child.

A new, rigorous approach to assessment was introduced, involving I.Q. testing of pregnant women considering adoption and the putative fathers where possible; full medical examinations of babies prior to placement; and calculation of life expectancy of prospective adopters by a medical adviser expert in life insurance. (Chapter 5 discusses I.Q. testing in greater depth.) This approach was seen by the professionals carrying it out as a world apart from the "cursory" checks and "hunches" which had been the feature of routine adoption practice before then. (McWhinnie, 1966, p. 2.) Adoption practice at the Guild of Service at this time was widely recognised to be of a high professional standard. (Younghusband, 1978.)

Other changes were equally significant in the professionalisation process. The system of record keeping was revolutionised. Gone were the daybook and card index, and in their place were case files. Each case now had its own file, and caseworkers were encouraged to keep full records of all contacts made, prefaced by a full case "history", which included all known information on the person's family background. At the same time, Dr McWhinnie devised a number of standard forms and pro-forma letters to cut down on time wasting and to ensure a general standard of service. This was particularly necessary because over this period and right through the 1960s, illegitimate pregnancies and adoptions dealt with by the agency were growing. Adoption placements escalated and continued to rise until a peak was reached in 1970. (See Figure 2.)

As the agency grew bigger, there were other internal changes necessary to fit with an increasingly professional, bureaucratic organisation. The style of social work intervention changed. Whereas before, caseworkers might have

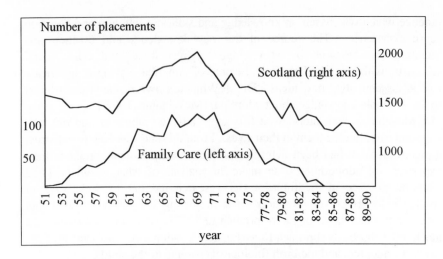

Source: Guild of Service/Family Care Annual Reports and Registrar
General for Scotland Annual Report, 1990, Figure T1.3.
General Register Office, Edinburgh.
Figure 2 Number of adoption placements
Guild of Service/Family Care and Scotland as a whole,
1951-1991

dropped in on clients at home, or clients come into the office "on speck",
now pre-arranged appointments were viewed as the proper way to meet
clients. And a formality appeared in the relationships between staff and
clients. Adoptive parents were always addressed as "Mr and Mrs", reflecting
a perceived difference in their status in relation to the agency. They were
never viewed as agency clients in the way that unmarried mothers were,[21]
and unmarried mothers continued to be called by their first names.

Another big shift at this time was in the agency's subjects, that is, in who
was allowed to carry out the social work task. What we see is a new splitting
of roles and tasks within the agency. This is evidenced in two ways. First,
volunteer committee members were gradually edged out of befriending
children at Edzell Lodge. It was no longer considered to be in their best
interests for committee members to take a special interest in individual
children, giving them cast off clothes, presents at birthday times, and taking
them out to tea. Working with the children became a professional task only,
and a new worker with a degree in Psychology was appointed to act as link
social worker between the caseworkers and the residential staff. The weekly
rotational visits of committee members to Edzell Lodge to hear about
management/administrative concerns (buying equipment, furnishings, staffing

matters) still continued, but committee members have expressed to me their sadness at being squeezed out of real contact with individual children. Some left the agency altogether. Others confined their activities to fund raising and serving in the Thrift Shop from then on.

But it was not only volunteers who found themselves excluded from areas of work. Amongst the casework staff themselves, two separate teams developed. Some caseworkers worked with single parents and unmarried mothers, (often the students, new workers and less qualified members of staff) and others worked with adopters (likely to be the better qualified staff). Whatever the rationale for this separation, the division led to feelings of a hierarchy in the agency, with adopters' social workers occupying some kind of privileged status in the agency.[22]

Stage three: professional consolidation and the challenge to professionalisation, 1962-1984

The next phase in the agency's life was at a general level one of consolidation. Miss Janet Lusk as new Director took over the professional sword from Dr McWhinnie in 1962 and carried the agency onwards and upwards. Janet Lusk strengthened the professional status of her agency and social work as a whole through her work on central and local government committees, professional associations, and innovative research projects. She attracted high quality staff to come to work at the agency, and struggled to get their conditions of service and salaries on a par with local authority employees. The agency had a high reputation for professional practice, and was called upon by voluntary and statutory agencies to give advice on systems and procedures, particularly in relation to its adoption work. Student placements in the Guild of Service were at a premium, as training for students in social work exploded nationally, and as courses and students fought to get training experience in such a good agency. (English, 1988, p. 119.)

Internally, professionalisation continued apace. As the agency grew, more staff were appointed. New senior staff came to take responsibility for supervising the practice of the "basic grade" social workers, leaving the Director time to develop contacts and practice outwith the agency. More secretarial staff were employed to free social workers to carry out their professional duties. This agency, along with all statutory social work expanded greatly, and the agency's funding base changed, as the agency progressively came to rely on government grants for the bulk of its financial support. (See Chapter Seven.)

Social workers were no longer expected to do any fund raising - this was definitely considered to be "unprofessional". At the same time, committee members' weekly management visits to Edzell Lodge were terminated, viewed as an unnecessary intrusion on the staff and the children in the home. These two seemingly small changes had one important consequence. Opportunities for staff and committee members to get to know one another and to value each others' contribution, already becoming difficult as the size of the agency grew, were reduced. Ex-committee members have described to me feeling excluded from the work of the agency, and resenting fund raising to pay increasing social work salaries rather than to support needy children.[23] Social workers, for their part, found the committee members out of touch and ill-informed, unsympathetic to the professional pressures.[24]

Anxiety about the distance between committee members and staff led to a decision in the mid 1970s to restructure the committees, giving senior social work staff voting rights on the Executive Committee for the first time, and abolishing the large General Committee, now viewed as an anachronism. The new model was intended to emphasise the partnership and co-operation between staff and committee members working together to establish agency policy and practice. In effect, some committee members saw it as a further incursion of professional social work power over lay committee members.[25]

But professional discourses in social work have not always succeeded over lay voices. As I have described in Chapter Three, committee members over-ruled a professional assessment in 1983 that a homosexual man should be passed as a prospective adopter. The decision was not only about homosexuality and parenting. It was about the lay committee members' right and duty to act as a brake on professional practice and to safeguard the agency's public standing. Not all lay committee members in fact disagreed with the social worker's recommendation, and not all social workers accepted it. But what happened was that it became impossible to hear the debate except as a professional versus lay disagreement. When Janet Lusk retired the following year, the new Director restructured the Executive Committee again, removing two senior staff members and reasserting the principle of a lay committee.

Challenges to the professional authority of social workers were not taking place only from lay committee members. There was also a significant and growing body of opinion from within social work which was highly cynical about the "fantastically pretentious facade" which called itself professional social work. (Wooten, 1959, p. 271.) Likewise, a number of voices were heard decrying social work's loss of its roots in the social reform movement. Towle (1961) was concerned that social work was losing "the cause" in favour of technique. She claimed that social workers were beginning to value their public image and their technical skills beyond the causes for which they should have been the advocates.

The 1970s witnessed two competing trends within social work, both of which will be described fully in Chapter 7. First, professional social work was strengthened to an unprecedented degree with the Social Work (Scotland) Act of 1968 (and the Seebohm Committee in England and Wales) and the emergence of local authority social work departments. Here the future pattern of professional social work was laid down. This was not to be an autonomous, private kind of professionalism as exemplified by private counsellors in the United States (and caseworkers in agencies like the Guild of Service), but what has been called a "bureau-professionalism". Professional control would now be established through the training of the vast numbers of unqualified workers in the employ of local authorities. (Parry et al, 1979, pp. 42-44.) And those employees brought a new challenge to professionalism as trade unionism began to have a significant voice in social work.

With the development of a radical movement within social work in the 1970s, professional social work in general and casework in particular came under attack. New ideas emanating from systems theory and the unitary approach brought back to centre stage the importance of *social* factors in assessment and decision making. New generic social work courses reflected this move away from individual, psycho-dynamic solutions, and away from specialist knowledge. And new approaches to social work practice were experimented with. Community work, group work and the use of volunteers became popular again, especially when these volunteers were from the same social class background, or had shared life experiences with those with whom they were working.

1973 marked the beginnings of the Volunteer Centre, set up to "promote current developments in volunteering and to foster the development of new opportunities for individual volunteers, voluntary agencies and community groups." (Volunteer Centre, 1975.) Research conducted in the early 1980s found that 1171 volunteers were working within sixty local authority social work teams throughout Scotland, mainly carrying out practical and befriending tasks. (Humphries, 1983.)

The Guild of Service (or Family Care as it became in 1978) was at the forefront of the development of some of the new approaches to social work intervention. Groups for single mothers, pregnant women and foster mothers were established with the appointment of a group worker in 1970. A volunteer befriending scheme for single parent families was initiated when a Volunteers Co-ordinator started work in 1973, and by 1976 volunteers were again taking children out from the children's home. But the agency held onto its insistence on professionalism throughout. It did not transform itself in the 1970s to become a self help or campaigning agency. The agency's volunteer scheme illustrates continued control by professional social work staff.

All referrals for volunteer befrienders came from social workers to the Volunteers' Co-ordinator, who was responsible for assessing volunteers, training volunteers, and matching volunteers to families or children in care. Thereafter, the relationship between the volunteer and client was monitored and reviewed at regular intervals. The nature of the assessment of volunteers mirrored that of adopters. A full background was taken, and as much as possible of the volunteers' attitudes and relationships was under scrutiny. The training itself drew on group psycho-dynamic principles in the early stages, later shifting to a much more pragmatic "preparation for volunteering" approach.[26]

In her report on the first three years of the volunteer scheme, Beth Humphries (Volunteers' Co-ordinator) points out the difficulty in integrating the scheme with the other work of the agency. She identifies a "polite and careful distance" being maintained by social workers, who gave only "lip service to the contribution of the lay person." (Humphries, 1976, p. 197.) Humphries later pursued this subject in a Ph.D. thesis on the ideologies of social workers and volunteers in statutory settings. Here she is critical of what she sees as the "colonised mentality" of volunteers in professional social work settings. She describes them as "oppressors and oppressed":-

> They were oppressed in that they were powerless to define themselves and their contribution, and their continuing as volunteers depended upon their acceptance of the professionals world view. They were oppressors in that they had become part of a social work professional ideology and as representatives of the Social Work Department were in a position to become carriers of dominant values and beliefs. (Humphries, 1983, p. 381.)

Although describing volunteers in statutory settings, there are clear echoes with volunteers in the Guild of Service/Family Care. Volunteers on the whole accepted their position in the hierarchy, and accepted professional assessments of children and families. But there has never been a total hegemony here. When two children were taken into care by a Family Care social worker in 1985, the children's volunteer accompanied their mother to the Children's Hearing which followed, and argued (successfully) that the children should be allowed to go home.[27]

The mid 1980s saw Family Care adopting a new approach to professionalism. Service users were encouraged to join committees (though significantly these tended to be adopters and volunteers rather than single parents); clients, committee members and social workers were encouraged to "join" Family Care and vote at Annual General Meetings; a new Policy Committee was formed to be the forum to which staff would take ideas and issues from their practice. Service users were also given permission to read their records for the first time, and new self help groups were established. Nevertheless, the main drive in the agency was still towards traditional professional social work discourse. When an Executive Committee member and agency volunteer made a passionate plea at the 1991 Annual General Meeting for the agency to expand its use of volunteers as the best way of solving the agency's financial difficulties, her advice was ignored. Faced by cut backs and severe financial stress, Family Care chose to retract rather than to de-professionalise its service.

Summary

Having set out carefully in the beginning to debunk uncritical acceptance of the idea of professionalisation as a smooth and steady development, I am nevertheless certain that something which we may call a process of professionalisation has been taking place in social work, and that this agency is a good illustration of this process. Throughout the professionalisation process a battle has been waged to determine what social work should be - what should be the limits and determining factors and rightful focus of concern of social work; who should be allowed to be social workers and to speak on behalf of social work; where social work should turn to draw its authority. (Foucault, 1972.)

The professionalisation contestation within Family Care was fought in the early years by different groups and individuals who were made up of the same social class and gender grouping. It was white, middle class women who fought amongst themselves to create not only a version of social work, but a way of acting as professional working women, with a professional status equal to that of their professional male colleagues. Increasingly, however, it was male academics and male psychiatrists/psychologists/ paediatricians who set the parameters of the debate within social work. And it was men who came to take over the top jobs when statutory social work provision expanded, and especially in the period post 1975 local government reorganisation when the powerful Regional Council social work departments were established. Family Care continued to reflect and illustrate professionalisation's progress, but it ceased to lead the field, or to anticipate any of the developments.

The professionalisation of social work cannot be isolated from the much wider context of a growing involvement of professionals operating on behalf of the state (whether working in statutory or voluntary agencies) and regulating the lives of families and individuals - the "psy" professions. (Donzelot, 1980.) It was the new legitimacy of intervention, and the huge explosion in statutory and voluntary social work which made possible and to a large degree necessitated a more rationally organised, bureaucratic, professional service. Psycho-dynamic theories and knowledge provided the underlying explanations for the shift.

In recent years, social work has shown some uncertainties in relation to its professionalising claims. As social work education has become more focused on the transmission of skills and tasks, so social work practice has become more regulated by central government legislation and local government rules and memoranda. At the same time, membership of the professional body British Association of Social Workers (BASW) is falling, and social workers have been unable to convince politicians or each other about the creation of a new General Council for social work. Bamford (1990) is sceptical about social work's professionalisation:-

> Twenty years after the Seebohm Report, social work has failed to establish its professional status, has a basic training shorter than that of other occupational groups involved in community care, and has dropped precipitately in public esteem. (Bamford, 1990, p. ix.)

I am left, finally, with feelings of ambivalence about the process of professionalisation in social work. I champion the rights of the early women social workers to be taken seriously and to work to create a status equal to that of male professionals (doctors, priests and lawyers). Nevertheless, I mourn the passing of some of the idealism of early social work, and I regret the exclusiveness of so much social work practice. We have created a vast empire for ourselves and will do anything we can to protect it from others - from volunteers, social work assistants, home helps, service users; in fact, from anyone who might grasp the reality that we have little more to offer than ourselves. This pattern seems set to continue, and perhaps even to worsen, as social work splits further between those elite social workers who manage care plans, and those less well qualified, less well paid care workers and volunteers who are responsible for delivering services.

Professionalism in today's social work is of a different kind to that envisaged by the early social workers. It is not about either professional autonomy or independence. It is about following legislation and guidelines; collaborating with others; and respecting service users. Consultation papers on the review of the Diploma in Social Work reflect the new managerialist, task-oriented style. Here the emphasis is stated as being to produce "national

84

occupational standards based on the concept of competence", and an extensive list of "units of competence" is offered as a way of providing a framework for teaching social work students. (CCETSW, 6 July 1994, p. 3.) Langan (1993) summarises the changes as follows:-

> It is no longer assumed that social work is almost a profession, able to understand and respond to the gamut of human misery. Rather, social work's claims to professional expertise lie in ruins. The "social work task" is increasingly fragmented, not merely in relation to different client groups, but into the functions of assessment, supervision, purchasing, management and care servicing. (Langan, 1993, p. 164.)

Notes

1. St. Agnes House was a training home for indoor and outdoor rescue workers and the central house of the Order of Divine Compassion, an Order of women who devoted their lives to rescue work.
2. Executive Committee minutes, 09-10-40.
3. Executive Committee minutes, 08-11-23.
4. Annual Report, 1933, p. 15.
5. Instead of "protecting women and girls against outrage, abduction and prostitution, and the terrible wickedness of the White Slave Trade", in 1930 the first Object became to "protect women and girls." Executive Committee minutes, 28-1-30.
6. The new first object became "to advise and befriend women and children by means of individual casework". Annual Report, 1946.
7. Interview, 26-03-90.
8. Interview, 15-03-90.
9. Annual Report, 1941.
10. This view also has been expressed to me by various respondents who worked during this period.
11. Interview, 15-10-90.
12. Lady Learmonth (1970), *Development of the Guild of Service* (unpublished paper), p. 3.
13. C.B. Learmonth (1965), *The Early Days of the Guild of Service and Edzell Lodge Homes*, unpublished paper, June.
14. Interview, 30-05-90.
15. Interview, 30-05-90.
16. Interview, 17-07-90.

Continued

17. Interview, 15-10-90.
18. Interview, 26-03-90.
19. In 1959, the first Object of the Association became:- "To provide a casework service for mothers and/or fathers (particularly the widowed, separated or divorced parent and the single parent) who have problems in relation to the care of their child or children especially where such a service is not available under a statutory provision or under another voluntary organisation." Annual Report, 1959.
20. Interview with Dr McWhinnie, 28-06-94.
21. Interview with Dr McWhinnie, 28-06-94.
22. Interview, 19-06-90.
23. Interviews, 22-10-90, 17-05-91, 29-05-91, 23-05-91.
24. Interviews, 26-02-91, 05-03-91, 04-02-91, 12-03-91.
25. Interview, 27-05-92.
26. Interview, 20-02-91.
27. Case file, 1985.

5 The psychiatric deluge?

Introduction

In her analysis of the development of social work in England and the United States, Kathleen Woodroofe (1962) claims that in America during and after the First World War (and a decade later in England) the social work scene was swept by a "psychiatric deluge which, for the time being at least, deflected social work into entirely new channels." She continues:-

> When it receded, it left rich alluvial soil in which new concepts were to take root and flourish, and older ones were to be vitalised and shaped anew. From these developments, especially from the teaching of Freud and his disciples, there was to emerge not only a new way of thinking about people, but an entirely new way of helping them. (Woodroofe, 1962, pp. 119-120.)

Woodroofe's notion of a "psychiatric deluge" has not gone unchallenged. Jones (1979) claims that the continuities within social work are more striking than the changes - that the take-up of Freudian theory "did not involve any fundamental shift in social work's stance or orientation." (p. 85.) Alexander's study (1972) of social work practice in the United States is equally sceptical about a North American "psychiatric deluge". He finds that "except in a few north-eastern cities, Freudian theory was not well known to social workers. Its influence was limited to an elite few rather then to the main body of the profession." (p. 538.) Yelloly (1980) provides a useful assessment. She argues that the impact of psycho-analysis has not necessarily been as direct as has been suggested. She proposes that social workers continued to be concerned with the impact of social issues such as unemployment, and that there was no "deluge" as such even in the United States. But she maintains nevertheless:-

> ... the adoption of a medical model of casework intervention with its tendency to focus attention on treatment processes in relation to the individual made a social or reform perspective more difficult to maintain. (Yelloly, 1980, p. 66.)

This chapter examines the influence of the psychiatric/ psychological/ psycho-analytic discourse (the "psy" discourse) on the social work scene in Scotland. Family Care exemplifies a social work agency which has lived through the changes associated with the development of psy principles within social work. At times in its history, Family Care has been in the forefront of these changes, pioneering intelligence testing and new casework methods, and training other organisations and social workers to adopt similar approaches. But Family Care has never been a centre of psycho-analytic expertise, either as a clinic or a therapeutic community. It therefore illustrates much more fully the partial nature of the "psycho-analysing" of social work - that is, the ways in which new ideas were adapted to fit specific circumstances and often to incorporate old ways of thinking about social work.

In this chapter I will look for evidence of the incorporation within social work of knowledge and methods which owed allegiance to a psychological or psycho-analytic perspective. I will be concerned to find out whether the psy influence has been as widespread and far reaching as has been suggested; what ideas were accepted while others were rejected; what older discourses survived alongside and intermeshed with the new conceptualisations. I will place this detailed picture in the wider context, giving consideration to the needs and aspirations which were served by the adoption of a new knowledge base, and the repercussions of its acceptance within social work. More specifically I will consider what kinds of subjectivity and solutions to social problems the psy discourse has made possible.

I will draw on two themes in my analysis. I will emphasise the constitutive role of knowledge, arguing that the new knowledge which social work adopted was a hybrid phenomenon which in turn made possible new ways of thinking about, speaking about and classifying social work and the social work task. (Foucault, 1972.)

I will also argue that the incorporation of the psy discourse was not accidental. Rather, it was a deliberate strategy on the part of social work educators and practitioners who were seeking a way of defining and organising social work which would distinguish it from every day common sense, and which at the same time would distance it from older, more punitive and moralistic discourses on social work. New ideas from psycho-analysis and psychology fitted the requirements of a professionalising service on both counts. (See Chapter Four.)

Social work was not, however, the only profession to adopt the new psy framework. The "psycho-analysing" of social work must be understood as part of a wider movement within society towards a more regulatory form of social control, administered and managed by the new psy professions, in which social work has played an important part. (Foucault, 1977; Donzelot, 1980.)

Definitions

Before getting immersed in the detail of the case study material, it is vital that some attention is given to definitions. I have already used a number of different terms without explanation - psychiatric, psycho-analytic, psychological, and psy.

Different writers have used these terms in different ways, to argue quite different points. Woodroofe (1962) exemplifies this confusion. She uses the terms "psychiatric" and "psychological" at times interchangeably, and at other times differentiated from one another. Although she writes about a "psychiatric deluge", in fact it is the influence of Freudian psychology (psycho-analysis, not psychiatry), which she sees as of greatest significance to the development of social work. When she fails to differentiate clearly between the two, this is in large measure because she believes that such distinctions are less important than the general movement towards what she calls "the science of the mind." (p. 126.)

Donzelot (1980) sees this very differently. He makes a clear differentiation between psychiatry and psycho-analysis. Psychiatry is described as a punitive technique of social control; it is control through institutionalisation/ hospitalisation and the use of force, with drugs playing a major part in controlling behaviour. Psycho-analysis, on the other hand, is assumed to have humanising potential. According to Donzelot, psycho-analysis is:-

> the only discourse on human psychism that was capable of placing an obstacle in the way of the racist and fascist representations that were generated by a psychiatry obsessed with eugenics. (Donzelot, 1980, xxiii.)

Donzelot identifies a series of phases in the development of social work, distinguishing between the psychiatric stage, which featured institutionalisation and the removal of problematic members from the family and the psycho-analytic stage, from the 1950s onwards, when the presenting problem was seen to be a *family* problem, and dealt with in the context of the family. Donzelot uses the term psy agency and psy specialist to refer to the host of counsellors, social workers, psychologists, and psycho-analysts who are involved in this practice of "non-degrading corrective action." (xxiv.)

Miller and Rose (1986) challenge the characterisation of Donzelot and others of "hard" psychiatry and "soft" alternatives - psycho-analysis, psycho-therapy, and "other talking cures". They see psychiatry and psychology as being involved in the same business, that is, in the regulation of individuals and their behaviour. From this perspective, the overlaps between psychiatry and psychology are more fundamental than the discrepancies between them - "the dependencies, interrelations and collaborations that have existed and continue to exist between them." (Miller and Rose, 1986, p. 3.)

Foucault (1977) is also concerned with the development of the "psy" complex. He identifies a shift in techniques of punishment from the surveillance of bodies to the surveillance of minds; from the control of the problem to the control of the problem-doer (the individual or the family); from a traditional form of law based on juridical rights to a colonisation by the psy complex and the criteria of "normalisation". He suggests that the new "social work" professions have a critical role to play in disciplining behaviour, through the process of hierarchical surveillance, normalising judgement and the examination. It is through this process that subjects and objects of the psy discourse are created. In effect, the discourse creates the categories which it then uses to classify and divide up people, and regulate and control behaviour.

It is this conceptualisation which I wish to foreground in my analysis of the impact of psychology/ psychiatry/ psycho-analysis on social work. I am not concerned with the debate over which discipline had the most significant impact at what period in history. Neither will I concentrate on the relative merits of one technique over another - psycho-analysis over psychology; psychology over psychiatry. Instead, I am interested to assess the *combined* impact of a psy discourse on social work. I will therefore use the term psy in a generic way to encompass all the ideas, theories and practices which are broadly derived from a psychological and psycho-analytic frame of reference.

The emergence of the psy discourse - the needs of children

It is to the 1940s that we must turn to find evidence of the beginnings of psy thinking and psy techniques in the work of the Guild of Service. Psy discourse emerged in the context of a major shift from vigilance to casework as the principal object of the agency, and most significantly, from women to children as the central focus of agency concern. This agency played a part both in building the new knowledge of child development, and in developing new ideas in practice with children.

The first reference to psy discourse in this agency can be found in the early 1940s. Miss Kay Stewart, the Organising Secretary, under the supervision and guidance of James Drever, Professor of Psychology at Edinburgh University, began a longitudinal study of the intelligence of illegitimate children and their unmarried mothers. Using Progressive Matrices (1938)[1] she tested the children at the point of entry into agency care - at first, this was foster care and after Edzell Lodge opened in 1947, on entry into the children's home. She re-tested them later to see whether she could prove the hypothesis that environment has a significant effect on children's intelligence.[2] Miss Stewart's research reflects both the rudimentary state of knowledge about children's development at this time, and the ways in which this knowledge base was being extended. The principal question being addressed was the relative importance of heredity over environment - which was more significant, and what were the implications for child care practice arising out of this?

Intelligence testing (psychometrics) was popular in Edinburgh from the 1920s onwards. A key figure in this work was Godfrey Thomson, joint Professor of Education at Edinburgh University and Moray House Training College, and James Drever's superior until Drever moved into the new Psychology Department in 1931. Thomson believed that hereditary intelligence was the principal variable in determining educational outcome. He therefore set about creating instruments for the measurement of intelligence and for building a coherent theory of functioning intelligence. His aim was to be able to provide educational opportunities which would "fit" children's potential, so that intelligent children would be stretched in their learning, and less gifted children would be given education appropriate to their level and ability.

Professor Drever's interests lay not with intelligence but with the measurement and understanding of personality, particularly with the impact of instincts on emotions. He devised character and temperament tests in the laboratory setting, and out of this work developed a theory of the bipolarity of emotion, which suggested a correspondence between personality and the fulfilment or thwarting of instinctive aims and emotions. (Sutherland, 1989.) He argued that the development of personality was related to the influence of environment on instinctual aims, and not to unconscious motivations or to inborn characteristics, such as intelligence.

Drever's interest in delinquency led him to take on court cases, and later behaviour problems and educational problems were brought to him for advice. By the early 1930s, Drever had his own out-patient clinic based at the Royal Edinburgh Hospital for children with behavioural and educational problems.[3] Miss Stewart played a key role in these developments. She was a founding member of the Child Guidance Council; in her position as court Probation Officer she referred "delinquent" children to Drever's clinic; and Professor Drever's assistant, Dr. Mary Collins was an Executive Committee member and life long friend of Kay Stewart.

The "heredity versus environment" debate was of course not confined to the Edinburgh scene. Psychology was building its professional status and scientific credibility on its claims to be able to measure individual differences and predict behaviour accordingly. Cyril Burt's work in London with delinquent boys and later with kinship groups also developed the debate between heredity and intelligence. He concluded that environment enhanced natural differences; hence the importance of testing all children.

There is not space or necessity to describe the whole field of psychometrics at this time. However, it is vital to have an awareness of not just the existence of this field of study, but some of its underlying implications and consequences. The psychology which held sway at this time was very much the psychology of the laboratory. Its instruments were technical, "scientific" ones, its practitioners were specialists, and its objects were individual differences. The solutions and strategies proposed followed on from this conceptualisation. Children were to be classified, divided up and treated according to these perceived individual differences. Rose (1985) argues that eugenic and neo-hygienist strategies came together in psychology. Individual psychology made it possible to diagnose and classify the feeble minded; to effectively divide up the population between those who could be treated/socialised/ educated and the residuum. (p. 85.)

The existence of psychometrics reflects a widespread concern about the general health of the population; about the falling birth rate, especially amongst the middle classes; and about the need to develop new approaches to welfare provision with the dismantling of the Poor Law. And psychology was itself striving at this time to achieve status as an independent science, equal in stature to other academic disciplines, by drawing on the methodology of physical science and the subject matter of moral philosophy. Foucault (1977) identifies the arrival of "individualising mechanisms" (like psychology) as an essential part of the shift away from punitive measures of social control towards the formation of a "disciplinary society". The focus on children as opposed to adults, on the sick rather than the healthy, on the mentally ill and delinquent rather than the normal and the non-delinquent is the process through which this transformation is achieved. (Foucault, 1977, p. 193.)

One of the most significant ways in which psy ideas influenced this agency was in the identification of the needs of children as separate from those of their parents. Although the agency had always concerned itself with the sexual protection of children, infants and children of unmarried mothers were seen largely as appendages of their mothers, rather than as agency clients in their own right.[4] During and after the Second World War, there is evidence of an increasing awareness of, and concern for the needs of children, and new agency services were begun as a consequence of this.

The Second World War played a major part in changing attitudes towards children. (Jordan, 1984.) The experiences of children in terms of evacuation, family breakdown and in residential nurseries were all under the spotlight. (Bowlby, Winnicott, Klein, Freud and Burlington all contributed to this explosion of interest in children.) The widely publicised death of a boy in foster care in 1945 focused attention on the personal social services for the first time. (Jordan, 1984.) There was a proliferation of literature and research, government reports and media attention focused on children, coming together in the Children Act of 1948.

The opening in 1947 of the agency's first children's home, Edzell Lodge, illustrates the new thinking about children. Miss Stewart had been concerned for some time about the experiences of illegitimate children boarded out in long term fostering placements. She was concerned about both the quality of care they were receiving, and also the difficulties for birth parents of maintaining links with their children.[5] There was also a great shortage of suitable placements. During the Second World War, the number of unplanned pregnancies had risen, and because of extra pressure on families (financial and practical), many foster parents had given up fostering. They had literally brought back to social work agencies the children for whom they were caring. An alternative provision had to be found.

Edzell Lodge reflected and anticipated some of the progressive thinking of the day, including ideas drawn from Adlerian psychology. Miss Stewart was a keen supporter of Alfred Adler, the first analyst to break with Freud and set up his own school of analysis. Adler minimised the importance of sexuality in the origin of neuroses. Instead, he introduced the concept of inferiority in determining future behaviour patterns. He claimed that all children experience feelings of inferiority, which, if handled positively, could lead to strong personal motivation and high achievement. When these feelings were too great to be satisfactorily overcome, for example in a person with "organ inferiority" (that is, physical defects or handicap), depression and neuroses might result. Adler believed that love and encouragement were crucial for young children in helping them to overcome their natural inferiority, as were the development of "social interest" (a concern for, and interest in others) and a reasonable degree of "activity". (Adler, 1924.)

Edzell Lodge was the first family group home in Scotland. It was set up as a resource for unmarried mothers: a place where the children of unmarried mothers could live and grow up, while still maintaining contact with their parents. A group of twelve children of all ages lived there, and others came to stay for short periods, for what we might today call respite care. Children attended the local schools, and were encouraged to get involved in their local community, taking part in clubs, and bringing friends home for tea. A nursery school was started in the Home, to be a place where children in the Home and in the community could mix and play together.

Edzell Lodge was revolutionary. It operated at a time when other "small" children's homes had up to fifty residents, dressed in uniform, and sometimes even referred to by numbers, not names. Miss Stewart acted as a committee member on the Clyde Committee on Child Care (Scotland's equivalent of the Curtis Committee in England and Wales) which promoted the idea of family group homes for the first time. People came from all over Britain to visit and learn from Edzell Lodge.

Even while Edzell Lodge was pioneering its new approach to residential child care, *all* residential care for children was under renewed scrutiny. Psycho-analytically derived work of Bowlby, Winnicott and others, with its emphasis on the significance of early childhood experiences for later adult maturity and the crucial importance the mother-child bond, forced a reassessment of child care, and of residential care in particular. (Bowlby, 1953.) Gradually adoption came to be considered the solution "in the best interests of the child", and the best adoptions were those carried out as early as possible in the child's life. The Guild of Service changed from being an agency which carried out adoptions only as a last resort in the 1940s to being an agency in the 1960s where adoption was the greatest part of its work.

The impact of psy discourse on casework

The early casework approach

In 1929 Miss Stewart described her approach to the casework of the agency:-

Before passing on any case to the appropriate Rescue Home or shelter, careful enquiries are made so as to make sure that the whole history of the case and any circumstances which may throw light on the future treatment are already known before definite steps are taken.[6]

The "history" referred to by Miss Stewart was not a psychological assessment of inner worlds or psychological depths. It was a practical assessment, an investigation of potential avenues of support, and possible difficulties ahead.

Miss Stewart's words are reminiscent of the Charity Organisation Society (COS) approach to casework. (Mowat, 1961.) The COS emphasised the need for a careful "scientific" enquiry which often included the taking up of references in order to make an "accurate" assessment of the client's likelihood of dependence or independence in the future. The assessment enabled the worker to decide whom to offer help to, and whom to leave to the vagaries of the Poor Law. The NVA worked along similar lines. Its main focus of attention was on those women deemed to be at risk, rather than on confirmed prostitutes who were unwilling to "give up their former lives."

Up to the late 1950s, there is no evidence in agency records or from my tape recorded interviews of any use of psycho-analytic terminology in the casework with women and children. The vocabulary used to describe the work contains no mention of "id" or "ego"; there is no hint of an interest in the relationship between the social worker and the service user; of hidden mental processes and unconscious motivations, or even of an interest in feelings to any extent.

Agency records leave no trace of the emotional side of the work. Case record cards state the brief facts - "baby went to Mrs X, foster mother." It is to the heart breaking letters which we must turn for evidence of the deep loss experienced by the women giving up babies. There are countless examples of letters written by birth mothers asking for progress reports on their children, and expressing at the same time deep gratitude to the caseworkers for making arrangements on their behalf. During interviews with me caseworkers accorded with my analysis of written material. They acknowledged that their work could be difficult and sad, but they did not express this in psycho-analytic terms, and had no knowledge and understanding of concepts such as "transference" or "insight".[7]

Neither was there any separation made between "presenting" and real (hidden) problems. The client was the unmarried mother; the problem was the unplanned pregnancy. This was very practical work. The caseworker was in effect a "manager" and a go-between, handling the negotiations and arrangements on behalf of unmarried mothers. It was the caseworker's task not only to make suitable arrangements for the first child, but to prevent further unwanted pregnancies. - (The policy of encouraging unmarried

95

mothers to maintain contact with, and to provide for the upkeep of their children was a large part of this strategy.) The client was defined in moral terms - she lacked "self control" and "discipline", or she had been exploited by an unscrupulous man. While attention was given to the physical needs of her baby (its need for clothing and shelter), there was little attention paid in the agency's early years to the emotional life of the baby, or to the relationship between the baby and its carers.

Psycho-analytic influence on casework with "unmarried mothers"

Case files from the 1960s and 1970s illustrate for the first time the direct application of selective psycho-analytic knowledge and ideas in the process of assessing clients' needs and problems. How well the caseworkers understood the terminology which they were using, and how far these were popular slogans or jargon is impossible to be sure. But there is evidence here that clients are no longer defined in moral terms. Instead, new psycho-analytic language is used to describe clients. A pregnant woman in 1968 is described as going through an "identity crisis"; another is said to have had a "neurotic illness in the past"; another in 1972 is described as being in a "phantasy situation". In many cases, the achievement of "insight" is held to be the primary goal in intervention.[8]

A general phenomenon throughout the case files is the ever present concern for the client's childhood and family background. Sometimes this attitude is expressed directly. For example, in 1968 a caseworker claims that the relationship between the pregnant girl and her parents "is vital in terms of becoming a secure adult".[9] More often, it is not put into words at all, but forms part of the value base and hidden assumptions from which the worker is functioning.

Agency assessment procedures enshrined the new conceptualisation of the importance of feelings, relationships and early childhood experiences. Case files included a full referral form, detailing not only the reasons for referral, but a family background or "history" which contained information about parents, siblings and the relationship with the putative father. The "taking of a history" was itself regarded as a potentially therapeutic exercise. This picks up a point I have made in Chapter 3 in relation to the links between psycho-analytic approaches and the confessional. Both set out to examine an "event" in detail. The main difference is that while the confessional focuses on the sinful act itself, psy techniques broaden this to an exploration of all thoughts and feelings connected with the act. (Foucault, 1976.)

The case notes which followed the history were lengthy descriptions of meetings with clients, and encompassed everything from factual details of the case to a great deal of impressionistic material about the client's feelings, the worker's feelings, and the relationship between the worker and the client. What the caseworker "thinks"/"believes"/"feels" was seen as relevant information, and there was a lot of attention paid to creating the "right kind of relationship" which would be satisfying to both the worker and the client.[10]

We can also see evidence of a shift in focus away from what were regarded as "presenting" problems (unwanted pregnancy, homelessness, poverty) towards "underlying" problems - the *real* problems, which may or may not be known to the client, but which the expert social worker or therapist was able to uncover. The social work literature of the time is full of assertions about the hidden motives of the unmarried mother. Leontine Young's (1954) study published in 1954 was a basic handbook for all agencies working in this field. Young argued that young women who had illegitimate children acted "purposefully". They wanted an out-of-wedlock child but not a husband, because they were emotionally sick and immature. The cause of this immaturity was held to be most frequently their mothers' domination of them.

The incorporation of psycho-analytic ideas into assessment may be regarded as something of a double edged sword. Clients would have had reason to be grateful that their behaviour was no longer judged as "bad" or "immoral", and it seems likely that the attention given to emotional and feelings aspects would have been experienced as generally positive and valuing. But the new approach to assessment implied that far more of the clients' behaviour was under scrutiny than before - their unconscious as well as their conscious motivations were open for examination and potential control.

Foucault (1977) describes the process of assessment as a "normalising gaze", a surveillance which makes it possible to qualify, to classify and to punish. This is not punishment in the conventional sense of physical punishment, but is the disciplinary punishment which Foucault regards as essentially corrective. (Foucault, 1977, pp.170-194.) The psy discourse allowed social work to create a whole new field of potential clients, those who were disturbed as well as those who were bad, and to introduce new techniques for helping and controlling them.

Yelloly (1980) states that social work never attempted to seriously carry out psycho-analytic treatment methods - dream analysis, free association, transference and interpretation. Psycho-analysis was never a realistic action theory for social workers. (p.163.) This perception is borne out by Family Care case material. Case notes overwhelmingly evidence the practical, down to earth nature of the social work task. However a caseworker might have chosen to conceptualise a case or set of underlying problems, the actual job itself entailed a high level of practical activities and arrangements, just as it had done in the earlier days of moral welfare. If the baby was to be placed for adoption, then the caseworker would be responsible for organising forms, medical examinations, intelligence tests, adoption panel meetings, collection of the infant, baby clothes. There would have been little time or opportunity for reflection or insight giving.

But there is another dimension here, that is, the client's ability to determine the service received. Social work intervention is *always* a negotiation and compromise between the social worker and the client. This is especially true in a voluntary social work agency where the contract between social worker and client is a voluntary one. It seems likely then that service users will have had the effect of mediating any potential excesses of psy casework. This is illustrated in a case from the early 1970s. A social worker fired with enthusiasm for Gestalt theory asked her client's permission to use Gestalt methods with her. The client agreed, but soon afterwards failed to keep appointments and for a time disappeared from agency view. Subsequent contact was of a practical nature, involving financial help towards a holiday for the client and her child.[11]

Another case reflects the gap between theory and practice in social work. A caseworker described to me in an interview the "fairly intensive psycho-dynamic work" she carried out with a single parent. She suggested that she had encouraged her client to look back to her own childhood to discover the origins of her present difficulties with her child, and to use the relationship with herself as caseworker to explore her relationships with others. (See Fairbairn and object relations theory, described in Sutherland, 1989.) When I examined the relevant case file, I found no record of this, and instead uncovered a steady stream of problems over electricity disconnection, eviction and another illegitimate pregnancy. This does not, of course, prove that the psycho-dynamic work had not happened. Rather, that it shows that it took place in the context of the practical, here and now crises which affected the life of the client - crises which had to be tackled at the same time as the more psy influenced work.[12]

Dr. Shenkin, a psychiatrist, addressing a conference on unmarried mothers in 1967 expressed the limitations of a psy approach:-

> The unmarried mother has to make many decisions and any technique which helps her to participate in these decisions is of special value. I would be wary of a routine psychiatric approach based on uncovering the infantile past at the expense of neglecting the real difficulties in the present. (Shenkin, 1967, p. 19.)

Other changes which effectively limited the opportunities for the development of psycho-analytic approaches in casework are related to the expansion of social services, and the increasing bureaucratic demands in the agency and in social work as a whole. One of the developments which accompanied professionalisation was an attempt to standardise the service - to create systems and procedures which all social workers would follow, and which would guarantee a certain minimum standard of intervention. Case files, systems of recording, practice procedures gradually reflected a much greater concern for regulatory, statutory and legal requirements than for emotional, or psychological techniques.

This trend has increased and become more prominent in recent years. Concerns about public disquiet and professional incompetence raised by a series of child abuse enquiries have prompted social work to stress much more the importance of following regulations and laid down procedures which may take little account of the psycho-analytic world of the client. Instead, the emphasis in the procedures has been on protecting the social worker and the agency from recrimination should things go wrong; ensuring that adequate and appropriate steps have been taken to prevent danger to the agency as well as to the child. At the same time there is a new emphasis on the language of rights.   Children's rights and parents' rights must be recognised and safeguarded. (Parton, 1991.)   The new world of contracts and the client as consumer of services which is promoted in community care legislation likewise fits very uneasily with psy approaches to assessment. (Griffiths Report, 1988.)

Specific examples of psy discourse in practice

Assessment in adoption

Adoption is one of the sites where psy ideas and practices are most apparent. By the 1960s about one in three women with illegitimate pregnancies gave up their babies for adoption, believing that this gave the babies a better start in life than they could provide themselves.   (McWhinnie, 1966). The new approach to adoption pioneered by Dr McWhinnie brought a "team" approach to adoption, highlighting medical, psychological, and social factors in adoption assessment and adoption placement. Dr McWhinnie urged the importance of "an objective appraisal of each individual situation", (1966, p. 5), that is, a thorough medical, psychological and social examination of the baby, the adopters, and the birth (biological) parents.

The principle client in all adoptions was deemed to be the child; the needs of biological parents and adopters were of secondary importance. From Dr McWhinnie's research, she argued that assessment was of vital importance in order to reduce risks of future emotional damage or adoption breakdown for the child. Assessment was about finding out as much as possible about all the parties concerned so that everyone could be appraised of the possible implications of what they were taking on:-

... we are not aiming at perfect prediction or backgrounds with no problems. We are simply saying, let us look at the background, and if there are risks which are recognisable, let us at least have the honesty and courage to know them, and to share them, where appropriate, with prospective adopters. (McWhinnie, 1966, pp. 25-26.)

It is important not to underestimate the radical nature of the Guild of Service's approach. At a time when adoption agencies were turning down babies with birthmarks, and accepting adopters on little more than references and good social standing, the Guild of Service carried out assessments as professional and "scientific" as possible.

Assessments of birth parents entailed a social worker's report, a medical report and an intelligence test. The social worker's report covered everything from family background to social circumstances and an account of how the pregnancy came about. Intelligence testing of birth parents was introduced in 1959 after consultation with Aberdeen University's Professor Rex Knight, an expert in the field. (Knight, 1950.) Tests used by the Guild of Service were the Hillside Short Form of the Wechsler-Bellevue Examination (a kind of general knowledge test and a conceptual performance test) and the Ravens Progressive Matrices (in which the aim was to carry out sixty puzzles to find the missing piece out of a collection of designs.) Advice in analysing results was supplied by a senior caseworker qualified as a Psychologist, in consultation with Professor Knight.

The test was viewed by social workers as particularly useful in situations where a mother had a very low intelligence, and was deemed to be borderline "mentally sub-normal."[13] The test was also believed to be a more reliable tool than a straightforward social worker's assessment of the client's potential, since the birth mother may have been working in a job below her capabilities, or simply reacting under stress and seeming less intelligent than she really was.[14]

The use of intelligence testing illustrates a number of underlying assumptions. First, we can see the belief that intelligence can be scientifically measured by specific tests of this nature. The present day critique of conventional intelligence testing suggests that tests may measure class and verbal articulacy rather than intelligence as such. (Vernon, 1979.)

A second assumption is that heredity is important. Children are believed to

100

inherit certain characteristics from their parents (including intelligence), and intelligence is seen as essentially stable throughout life; hence the usefulness of testing of biological parents as a predictor of the intelligence of their children. Moreover, contemporary research held that the mother was more important than the father in determining the child's inherited intelligence.[15]

Intelligence testing was used for only a short time at the Guild of Service. By the mid 1960s, the agency moved away from testing in favour of a more open ended assessment by social workers. This was in part in recognition of the fact that there was a growing unease amongst agency social workers about the process of testing. Some found the testing "arrogant" and felt uncomfortable about doing the tests.[16] More crucially, questions were being asked in the agency and beyond about what the assessment process was for - "there was no use constructing elaborate selection procedures if we didn't know what we were *selecting for.*"[17]

This takes me to the assessment of the adoptive parents. Conventional adoption practice at this time centred on an interview, a G.P.'s letter, and a letter of recommendation, often from a clergyman. The Guild of Service, basing their ideas on Dr McWhinnie's research findings (1967), introduced a much more rigorous assessment, which included a medical assessment of the couple's life expectancy, a psychiatric report, and a full social history taken by the social worker. The social worker concentrated not just on age, family pattern, and education, but on relationships and attitudes, particularly on attitudes to illegitimacy and infertility. As Dr McWhinnie writes:-

> (Couples) have found it reassuring that discussion of their intimate attitudes and relationships, with social workers understanding the significance of these, has contributed to a much more secure foundation for adoptive parenthood. (McWhinnie, 1966, pp. 28-29.)

Assessment of adoptive parents provides a clear illustration of a new role for the psy professionals in terms of disciplining behaviour. (Foucault, 1977.) What the new methods made possible was not just a greater predictability of success in adoption, or a better "match" in adoption, but rather, greater control over the adoption process, and of the adopters themselves. As new knowledge about the importance of relationships and attitudes came to influence practice, so more of the adopters' lives came under scrutiny.

But adoption practice did not stand still. We can soon see competition taking place between different sets of psy ideas and practices. As social work moved away from the search for the "absolutes" of psychometrics and intelligence testing, so it looked sympathetically towards new ideas emanating from behaviourism and social learning theory. By the mid 1960s, the concept of "selection" for adoption was shifting towards the seemingly more egalitarian notion of "preparation" for adoption.

This new approach, developed in the United States and pioneered by the Kirks on a lecture tour of Britain in 1967 (Kirk and Kirk, 1966) argued that psycho-analytic theories, although useful in giving insight into past events, were *not* predictive. Hence they could not be used to determine what kind of adoptive parent an individual would make. They argued that it was better to concentrate on the preparing and educating of people for their future roles as adoptive parents, instead of on the screening (selection) of applicants.

At the same time, the idea that a "match" between adopters and child was feasible or even desirable in adoption was itself under scrutiny. Attempts to place children with parents of similar colouring/ physique/ background and intelligence were discredited on the basis that they led to unrealistic expectations and attitudes on the part of adoptive parents, and encouraged a denial of the child's origins and past.[18]

Social work did not take on board these new concepts in a vacuum. They were social work's way of coming to terms with, and keeping up with the socio-economic and cultural changes which were taking place within the client group and within society. Already by the mid 1960s, the supply of healthy white babies for adoption was showing signs of decreasing. As contraception and abortion became more readily available, and as it became financially more viable and morally more acceptable to choose to be a single parent, the trend towards decreasing numbers of babies being placed for adoption continued. Although overall adoption figures remained high in this agency until the late 1960s (see Chapter 4, Figure 2), "hard to place" children took up an increasing proportion of these cases. Adoption placement of "hard to place" children (some of whom had medical problems, others who were black or mixed race, and others who were older children) meant that old methods of selection and matching no longer worked, and new procedures had to be found. (See Figure 3.)

Residential work with children

There was one setting where psycho-analytic techniques were experimented with, that is, the residential setting. It is to Edzell Lodge in the 1970s that we must turn to find deliberate attempts to turn new psy ideas and theories into practice - ideas drawn from the contemporary psy preoccupations with behaviour modification, psychotherapy, psychodrama and transactional analysis.

By the 1970s, Edzell Lodge was no longer providing a stable long term residence for a small group of children. Instead, it provided Social Work

Year	White healthy babies	Hard to place children	Total
1955	0	30	30
1960	2	38	40
1965	5	63	68
1970	5	85	90
1975	10	59	69
1980	17	9	26
1982	6	0	6

Note: The agency stopped placing babies for adoption after 1980 when it was decided by Lothian Region Social Work Department that all baby adoptions would be handled by Scottish Adoption Association. Adoption placement ended completely after 1982 when the Social Work Department itself assumed responsibility for all "hard to place" children. Family Care developed an Adoption Counselling Centre as an alternative service.

Source: Guild of Service/Family Care annual reports and adoption case-books.

Figure 3 Hard to place adoptions, Guild of Service/Family Care, 1955-1982

Departments from all over Scotland with a unit which prepared troubled and troublesome adolescents to move on, either back to members of their original family, or on to a new adoptive family. All these children had chaotic and disrupted pasts. Some were already acting out in delinquent ways; all were seen as difficult, emotionally damaged children.

While at Edzell Lodge, the children worked with residential staff and social workers on "life history books", building up a picture of their past and present lives. They also worked in groups with other children, using role play, puppets, and arts and crafts materials as ways of getting in touch with feelings and acting out and rehearsing new situations. The general environment of the Home was intended to be as "free" as possible. Children were encouraged to express their feelings and, if necessary, to temporarily "regress" - babies' bottles, comfort blankets and toys ("transitional objects") were widely used. There was no physical punishment in the Home. Instead, "token economy" systems such as star charts were introduced as reinforcers of desired behaviour, for example to help with bed wetting. (See Jehu, 1972.) Really difficult behaviour was dealt with either by withdrawing privileges such as pocket money, or "holding" children until they came out of a temper tantrum.

Underpinning the work was an assumption that there is a normal, healthy pattern of development in childhood, and that children who have for some reason been unable to develop need time to go back before they can recover emotionally. There was also a strong belief in the therapeutic value of play. Play was seen as purposeful, and related to the child's inner mental and emotional processes. (Basic texts on residential care used by staff included Dockar-Drysdale, 1968 and Balbernie, 1966.)

Significantly, all this psy based activity was carried out under the supervision and support of child psychologists and psychiatrists from the Royal Hospital for Sick Children in Edinburgh who visited on a regular basis to discuss individual children and to lead staff training sessions. Social workers were not themselves expected to be the psy experts.

The experience of Edzell Lodge underlines the eclectic nature of social work; the way social work reflects a mixture of ideas and practices, old and new. Here we can see new psycho-analytic language and method alongside older, resilient notions about child care, notions which upheld values such as respect for authority, politeness and good manners, discipline, Christian observance, and service to others. Edzell Lodge up until its closure in 1984 never became a permissive, free living therapeutic community like Summerhill. (Neill, 1962.)

The psy discourse and social work - psy under siege?

Even supposing we accept that there was a time when psy ideas were prominent in social work in Britain, this period was undoubtedly short lived. By the 1960s and 1970s there was an attempt to bring together various strands into one "unitary" approach based on a theoretical framework drawn from systems theory. (See Parsons, 1951; Pincus and Minahan, 1973, Specht and Vickery, 1977.) Here environmental ideas were put together with psy notions to reach an understanding of human behaviour based on a conceptualisation of interconnecting systems of family, community and society. Change was now related to planning and structuring of goals through a "problem solving" approach, rather than through the giving of insight as an isolated activity. Bamford (1990) describes the realities of social work practice, particularly in statutory settings:-

> Casework in the sense of a therapeutic relationship stretching over months and years was a luxury which the public sector was unable to afford under the bombardment of referrals. (p. 9.)

By the 1970s, radical social work theory and practice (see Bailey and Brake, 1975) and later feminist theories criticised social work for being pathological, class ridden, and part of the social control mechanisms of society. Solutions were to be found in making alliances with working class clients and with women, by working with them in their communities to provide the services they required; to empower them to make effective demands and to challenge the status quo. Community work approaches and group work were held to be more helpful in this context than casework with individuals and families.

Social work as it is carried out in statutory and voluntary organisations today reflects a host of different assumptions and ideas. In spite of attempts to create a generic social work practice, social work remains a variable activity, with its theoretical and ideological roots in a wide variety of discourses. For many social workers, psy ideas have been relegated to background material; useful in understanding values and attitudes, individual motivations and causes of behaviour, but less central to actual social work practice. Task centred, short term intervention approaches are in vogue, along with a strong emphasis on the practical, administrative and management aspects of social work. This is illustrated by the new emphasis on achieving "competencies" in social work education; on outcomes rather than process in learning to be a social worker. (See CCETSW Paper 30, 1989.) At the same time, the bureaucratic, legalistic language of child protection and case management places far more stress on contracts and procedures than on relationships and insight. (Parton, 1991.)

Nevertheless, psy discourses are remarkably resilient, and individual social workers and specific social work agencies still draw on psycho-analytic and psychological material for their assessments and their practice. Family Care social workers in the 1980s and 1990s drew on new feminist psychological approaches in their work, and techniques of transactional analysis were adapted for use with clients. (See James and Jongeward, 1971.) The work of Carl Rogers remains popular in social work, and forms the basis of much counselling in social work. (Rogers, 1951, 1980.) Social learning theory is widely used today in learning programmes with groups of clients - with men in prison, with men who have been violent to their partners, and with women survivors.

The recent expansion of counselling services illustrates the persistence and success of the psy discourse. New expert counselling services have been set up to provide counselling to individuals and families undergoing a range of personal dilemmas and problems. We have abortion counselling, adoption counselling, bereavement counselling, marital counselling, divorce counselling, infertility counselling, and now disaster counselling. Some of these services are run by private and voluntary agencies. Others are institutionalised into the state mechanism and required by law. Smart (1989) identifies the increasing extension of psy as part of new disciplinary mechanisms in society, regulated by law. She illustrates this with a discussion of the recommendation by the Warnock Committee (1984) that infertility counselling should be made a requirement for all those receiving infertility treatment. (pp. 90-113.) Legislation did follow this course. Hospitals offering in vitro fertilisation are under a statutory obligation to offer "implications counselling", that is, counselling which explores the medical issues involved and the immediate consequences for couples. While some of this counselling may be provided by medical staff (as in the case of abortion), there is increasing pressure for more specialist, trained counsellors to carry out this work, and social workers are promoting themselves as the counselling experts in this situation.[19] Family Care, anticipating the new legislation, set up a counselling service in 1991 for all couples receiving AID (artificial insemination by donor) at the Western General Hospital in Edinburgh.

Summary

I am clear that there was no simple "psychiatric deluge" in social work in Scotland in the 1950s or at any other time. The psy perspective which informed and negotiated with the social work task between the 1930s and 1970s was not a pure discourse. It contained selective borrowings from psychology (principally psychometrics and social learning theory and behaviourism) and from psycho-analysis (including concepts from competing psycho-analytic schools, and from offshoots of psycho-analysis such as existential or humanist psychology and interactionist psychology.) It ignored psycho-analytic and psychological ideas which did not fit or seem useful, such as perception or the sexual instinct. And its take up was quite patchy and arbitrary. It was dependent upon current teaching on social work courses; on the professional preferences of individual social workers and social work managers; and on the views of the lay members who sat on committees in the agency and monitored agency practice. It was dependent too upon clients' willingness to accept psy based intervention. Just as importantly, it had continuities with the old styles which it sought to replace.

What the psy discourse did however was to provide an explanatory framework and a set of ideas which effectively lifted social work knowledge and skills out of the realm of "common sense", everyday knowledge and skills. It provided a sense of expertise which social workers, intent on upgrading their work, were seeking. Social work, psychology and psycho-analysis were all struggling at this time to have their status and their theories recognised and accepted in the professional world inside and outside their disciplines. For social work, this meant rejecting existing theories and methods as "unprofessional", and laying out clear boundaries about who was, and who was not allowed to practice social work - in Foucault's language, "who is allowed to speak?" The impact of psy discourse on social work was to justify and extend professional boundaries and professional claims. While these claims were never totally successful or unchallenged, their influence was extensive. This process continues, with a current drive to insist that all residential and day care social workers should have professional social work training and qualifications; nursing qualifications are no longer considered adequate.

The psy discourse also had a specific role to play in enabling a shift to take place both in the "objects" of the social work discourse and in the "strategies and solutions" which it set out to achieve. Put very simply, the psy discourse smoothed the transition taking place between the adult as object to the child. From the mid 1940s onwards, children's needs came to be seen as separate from parents' needs for the first time; children were seen as individual, psychological beings differentiated from their parents. Aligned with this was a set of assumptions about what children's needs were, and how best these could be met. Families were held to be best for children, and special kinds of families at that - that is, with two parents, and with mother as primary carer, based at home. The policy changes in adoption and residential work in Family Care bear witness to this change.

What the psy discourse made possible, above all, is a specific way of understanding human beings and human problems. Jones (1979) argues that psycho-analytic theory permitted a shift to a "softer" approach to problem families who had earlier been considered as part of the irredeemable and undeserving residuum. (p. 86.) There is evidence that psy discourse in social work may have encouraged social workers to sympathise with clients more, and judge them less. (A social worker from the mid 1980s coping with a child abuse case described her work as "nurturing" women. She saw herself as the "loving parent these women had never had".[20]) But the psy discourse, offering as it does explanations based on individuals and individual problems will always be a conservative discourse. It sets out to fit people to society, not to change society.

Psy discourse has legitimated a greater degree of state interference in family life through welfare and social work agencies, what Foucault refers to as "disciplinary networks" (Foucault, 1977, p. 306), on the principle that if children could be socialised from an early age, then the costly cycle of deprivation could be broken. This can be interpreted positively and negatively. While neglected and abused children are more likely to be brought to the attention of social work and the state, so more children and families are caught up in the welfare net. This is the central paradox of preventive child care - the twin strategy of the "policing" of families. (Donzelot, 1980.)

Notes

1. Progressive Matrices (1938), prepared for the Research Department, R.E.C.A., Colchester.
2. Miss Stewart's research was never completed, and no written records remain which evidence this work.
3. Information from *A History of Psychology in Autobiography Volume II*, (1932), Clark University Press, London.
4. Interview, 26-03-90.
5. Interview with Miss Stewart, 17-07-90.
6. Annual Report, 1929, p. 8.
7. Interviews, 26-03-90; 20-04-90; 17-07-90.
8. Case records, 1960s and 1970s.
9. Case record, 1968.
10. Case records, 1960s.
11. Case records, 1972.
12. Interview, 02-05-91.
13. Interview, 05-02-91.
14. Interview, 04-05-90.
15. Correspondence with social worker, 01-06-90.
16. Interview, 19-06-90.
17. Correspondence with social worker, 01-06-90.
18. Correspondence with social worker, 01-06-90.
19. R. Siddall (1994), "Baby Talk", *Community Care*, 3 March.
20. Interview, 13-03-91.

6 Women and the social work task

Introduction

> Social work has, since the war, played an expanding and highly ideological role. Its emphasis has been directly on the reinforcement of traditional forms of family life; this has in fact been its main purpose within the constellation of welfare services and the reality behind its official role ... (Wilson, 1977, pp. 83-84.)

> ... while (social) work consistent with feminist aims can be carried out, it remains a minority activity set alongside the dominant routines of practice constantly reinforcing the sexist nature and social control role of statutory social work. (Dominelli and McLeod, 1989, p. 16.)

The above quotations capture the substance and the spirit of the prominent feminist critique of social work's role within the welfare state. Social workers are presented as actively creating and maintaining women's oppression through the upholding of traditional family values and a patriarchal social order. Social work is described as fundamentally sexist and at the same time gender blind, failing to see the unfair burden it places on women in the family.

So where does this leave those of us whose careers have been spent working within social work? Is it ever possible to carry out social work which is non-oppressive to women, and which might even succeed in empowering women? And what about those who have gone before? Are we the first generation of social workers to properly understand the nature of the relationship between women and social work? Or have women struggled with the inherent dilemmas ever since there was something called social work?

This chapter sets out to answer some of these questions, by looking in depth at the relationship between women and social work in the context of the history of Family Care. I will examine women in their role as service providers, managers and service users, over an eighty year period. I will argue that while social work is sexist, it is not only sexist - that is not the sole reason for its existence. At the same time, I will suggest that although social work as an institution inevitably controls and directs women, it also has the capacity to support and empower women, as clients and as staff members; and that care and control are not, and have never been institutionally separate in social work.

But here is another important point. The interests of women social workers may not always be the same as those of women clients. A historical approach highlights that there are a number of competing discourses which address women in social work - discourses which operate at times against one another and at times together, sometimes working to oppress women and sometimes to support and empower them. The relationship between women and social work can only be understood as a place of intersection between different discourses, the two most prominent of which are feminism and famialism. By unpicking the feminist and familialist strands within social work over the three key periods - the vigilance period, the post war period, and the 1970s onwards - we can see the reality of the contradictions inherent in the social work task, which is sexist (as well as classist and racist), and yet also has the scope to support women's interests and women's concerns.

The context - women and men in social work

The fact that women have always played a central role in social work, as providers and recipients of services, has been well documented. (Walton, 1975; Davis and Brook, 1985.)

Women have been particularly important in agencies like Family Care - a voluntary agency which focused on "women's issues", that is women and children at risk, unmarried mothers, and single parent families, again, most frequently, single mothers and their children. Between 1911 and 1991, Family Care employed only two male social workers amongst hundreds of women social workers. All its Directors and senior social workers have been women, although a male Secretary/ Treasurer has been in post for ten years. Committee members have largely been women, especially in the period post 1945, and strenuous efforts have been made over the last few years to redress this "imbalance."

The under-representation of male social workers in the organisation is partly attributable to the nature of the work. Because most of the agency's clients have been women and children, the work has always attracted a higher proportion of women social workers. This matches the wider experience in social work. Historically men were more likely to be found in settings which required a measure of "control" - as probation officers, school attendance officers and civil servants, while women were found in more "caring" roles - child care, almoning and of course, moral welfare. (Walton, 1975.)

But there is another contributing factor. This agency, at the forefront of professional social work in Scotland, chose only the best qualified candidates for its vacant posts, and these historically were women. The agency did not set out to employ women in preference to men. It was simply that until comparatively recently women were the best candidates.[1] A career in social work up until the 1960s was traditionally the prerogative of educated middle class women denied access to other professional occupations. Some were married and could employ domestic help at home; others were unmarried and devoted their lives to their work. (Davis and Brook, 1985.) Those men who did enter social work included those who had been unsuccessful in conventional "male" career routes, and may therefore have been less well qualified.

Good male candidates would undoubtedly have been put off by lower pay and career advancement opportunities (internal promotions, external job transfers) in the voluntary sector. Certainly the establishment of statutory social work in Scotland after the Social Work (Scotland) Act of 1968 led to an influx of men into senior management posts in social work, including a number of men from outside Scotland who grasped the opportunity for career advancement posed by this and later local government reorganisation in 1975. Voluntary agencies like Family Care struggled to reach a position where social workers' pay and working conditions met those of local authority departments. The Director's post at Family Care remained at senior social worker grade until the Director retired in 1983, when her salary had to be vastly uprated to attract good quality applicants. The resultant short list for the post unsurprisingly contained four men and one woman. The woman candidate was appointed, on the basis of merit, not gender.

Although the agency found it difficult to match the salary and conditions of service of the local authority Social Work Departments, there was a time when its working conditions were in fact in advance of those of the statutory services. The Guild of Service gave its Director maternity leave in the early 1960s - a quite unheard of arrangement, at a time when many local authority departments refused even to employ married women.[2] The Guild of Service, in choosing to employ married women, also took an enlightened approach to part time working. Hours of work wherever possible were negotiated to suit workers' commitments to dependent relatives (children and parents), and as a result a high proportion of the staff were part time workers.

The entry of married women into paid employment is one of the major post war social and economic changes which have taken place. Between 1951 and 1981 the number of economically active women in Scotland rose by thirty eight per cent, while the number of men fell by about nine per cent. McCrone (1992) suggests that the single most important shift has been the arrival of married women into the work force. And while married women have entered paid employment, so part time work has increased.

The changing gender balance of committee membership illustrates another shift taking place in social work as a whole. (See Figure 4.) During the early years of the NVA, men and women were equally represented on committees. This was indicative of two factors. First, vigilance work - that is, protecting women and children and changing sexual behaviour - was seen as equally pertinent to men and to women. Second, women and men were regarded as having unique and differing contributions to make to the agency's work.

Year	Men	Women	Total
1911	8	8	16
1916	8	8	16
1921	4	10	14
1926	3	11	14
1931	5	10	15
1936	5	10	15
1941	2	12	14
1946	2	17	19
1951	1	12	13
1956	1	13	14
1961	0	17	17
1966	0	21	21
1971	0	21	21
1976	2	13	15
1981	3	15	18
1986	5	8	13
1991	5	6	11

Source: NVA/Guild of Service/Family Care Annual Reports.

Figure 4 Gender balance of executive committee, NVA/Guild of Service/Family Care, 1911-1991

Men's "rationality" and legal knowledge were balanced on committees by women's greater understanding of "human affairs".

Prochaska (1980) describes the nineteenth century tradition of women and men working together on philanthropic bodies, often (but not always) with men at the helm, and with women carrying out key functions on behalf of the agencies. As well as serving on committees, women worked as visitors, inspectors and befrienders of the poor, the sick and the imprisoned. Women who became involved in public life stressed that they were bringing feminine qualities into a male world - bringing "the mother spirit into politics".[3] They also saw a correspondence between their voluntary work and their domestic responsibilities. For example:-

> Poor Law work is specially fitted for women; for it is only domestic economy on a larger scale. Accustomed to regulate her own house, a lady has had precisely the training necessary to fit her for a Poor Law Guardian ...[4]

After the First World War, men's participation on committees dropped considerably - there were less men available to get involved in voluntary work of any kind, and as I have described in Chapter 2, the NVA found it difficult to attract new recruits to the vigilance cause. After the Second World War, men's involvement changed completely. Instead of sitting on committees, they left this to their wives and mothers, and became professional advisers, called in to give specific guidance on individual cases, or legal or financial help when needed. Between 1960 and 1976, the Executive Committee (the main policy and decision making body) was an all female committee, made up largely of the wives of the Edinburgh upper middle classes. Respondents have told me that women considered that they had "made it" into Edinburgh society when they were appointed to the Executive Committee of this agency.[5]

By the mid 1980s committee membership had changed again. Women and men became more equally represented, but this time they were all professionals in their own right, representing other agencies or other disciplines. The "knowledgeable housewife" disappeared completely from committee management, to be replaced by the professional with "expert" knowledge and experience. (See Chapter 4.)

To re-cap, Family Care is an agency in which women and men have both had a part to play, but in which women have been the central focus, both as givers and receivers of services. This corresponds with the historical picture of women's participation in social services throughout Britain, with the one major difference being that women here retained their hold on senior posts.

Definitions - feminism and familialism

Feminist/feminism

Definitions of "feminist" and "feminism" are very much open to question, and are difficult to pin down when applied historically. The terms "feminist" and "feminism" arrived in Britain from France in 1895, and have been used in different ways ever since.

Some feminist writers argue that only those women who are consciously feminist in their actions and values can be considered to be feminists. Feminist historians tend to prefer a broader definition. Banks (1981) asserts that "any groups that have tried to change the position of women, or ideas about women, have been granted the title feminist." (p. 3.) Similarly, Bland (1987) uses the terms retrospectively to refer to "thoughts, actions and persons that challenged the existing power of men over women and its consequent inequalities." (p.142.)

I will use the terms "feminist" and "feminism" in this inclusive sense, to encompass behaviour and attitudes which uphold and promote the rights of women, but which may not be self-consciously feminist in definition. This is vital if we are to understand the strongly pro-women messages implicit in the deeply conservative vigilance discourse. It also reminds us that "feminism" is and always has been a broad movement, which contains a diversity of philosophy and strategy within a general aim to better women's position in society.

Banks (1986) in an analysis of the social origins of the early feminist movement identifies three very different ideologies and traditions in feminism - "equal rights feminism", with its roots in the Enlightenment; "the evangelical movement", which emphasised the need to give women's special and unique qualities more significance in public life; and "socialist feminism" which was to become the main strand within feminism at the end of the nineteenth century, placing its faith on the development of the welfare state. (pp. 6-7.)

Feminism today has a number of different and competing strands. Socialist feminism, radical feminism, separatist feminism, Marxist feminism all co-exist and compete to be heard inside and outside the feminist movement. (Delmar, 1986.) While the Women's Liberation Movement of the 1970s sought to reduce and deny differences between women, feminists today debate the validity of a woman's or feminist standpoint/ standpoints. We are faced with the complex reality of women's differences, and in particular our unequal experience of oppression. Ramazanoglu (1989) expresses this in terms of "contradictions of oppression", contradictions which are to do with our shared experience of living in society, and yet our differential experience of oppression based on social class, educational background, sexual orientation, disability.

These contradictions will be abundantly clear in the history of Family Care. The feminists who fought for the vote and for women's right to refuse unwanted sexual contact were the very women who employed (exploited?) working class women as domestic servants, and sought to control the freedom of movement of women and children of all classes. I am myself one of the feminist social workers whom I will describe influencing the agency's work in the 1980s. Our feminism reflected much of the idealism of the Women's Liberation Movement, particularly the sense of shared sisterhood. And yet faced with the overwhelming needs of the children with whom we were working, this approach had to be compromised.

Familialism

Familialism is the second key discourse which has addressed women within social work. Familial ideology or familialism can be described as the belief that a women's role is principally that of wife and mother, and that the heterosexual, nuclear family is the natural and normal way to bring up children.

Feminists writing in the 1970s and 1980s initiated a major re-think about the family, identifying it as a major site of, if not the source of, women's oppression. (Beechey, 1985, p. 101.) Elizabeth Wilson was in the forefront of the feminist critique of the family, and of the welfare state. She argued that familial ideology, with its roots in the history of welfare, became much more prevalent after the Second World War. It was at this time that psychologists, sociologists and government reports all pushed the nuclear, heterosexual family as the norm. The welfare state was set up, in her view, to embody and promote familial ideology; the primary function of social work was to reinforce traditional forms of family life. (Wilson, 1977.)

Wilson has been criticised for presenting too functionalist an account of the workings of capitalism and of social work's role within it. Riley (1983) challenges the assumption that post-war familial ideology was a concerted drive to force women to give up work and go back home to raise the next generation of children. She indicates that different factors operated after the war in quite a contradictory fashion, and that the connections between government plans, the movements of women on and off the labour market and the development of psychological beliefs were "far more fragile than feminist interpretations generally allow." (p. 11.)

McIntosh (1979) claims that neither the family nor the oppression of women is eternal and unchanging - they have to be understood in all their historical

115

complexity. She points out that although state policy may seek to bolster the system of the family household, a growing number of families do not in fact fit the state's assumed family arrangement (that is, a nuclear family with husband at work and dependent wife at home.) As a result, there is a constant struggle over how best to meet the needs of those who are outside this arrangement (the elderly, the sick, the long term unemployed.)

I find the notion of familial discourse (encompassing the beliefs, concepts, and ideas which govern action) a useful way of conceptualising the complex processes at work here. Although Foucault spent little time examining the family, he did nevertheless identify the family as playing a central role in the control of sexuality and sexual deviance. (Foucault, 1976, p. 112.) Donzelot (1980) has drawn on Foucault's conceptual framework to develop a historical analysis of the relationship between the family and the state.

Donzelot characterises the family as an ever changing form, a mechanism through which other agencies operate and a site of intersections rather than a pre-given institution. He identifies the development in the late eighteenth and early nineteenth centuries of a sector which he defines as "the social" - neither public nor private, independent from and connected with other sectors (juridical, educational, economic and political). Then in the twentieth century, according to Donzelot's characterisation, a new series of professions assembled under a common banner - "social work" (social workers, teachers, health visitors, youth workers) - to take over the mission of "civilising the social body." (p. 96.) Donzelot suggests that psycho-analysis became the tool which was to complete the shift - the "psy" was instrumental in the process of weakening the power of the family through the widespread diffusion of a "familialism" which upheld and reinforced the realm of the social. He identifies a contemporary situation in which "the family appears as though colonised" - that is, there is what he refers to as "a patriarchy of the state". (p. 103.) (I discuss this more fully in Chapter 5.)

I find Donzelot's conceptualisation of the dynamic nature of the family very informative, though I am wary of his value position on this.[6] Women have indeed chosen to intervene to change the relations between men and women in the family. And the family has quite clearly become more "policed" in recent years by educational, psychological and legal discourses which define and regulate the behaviour of family members. But I doubt that the policing of families has been as total or conclusive as Donzelot may seem to suggest. On the contrary, I aim to show that the social work task betrays an acceptance of many different kinds of families, and that control over families by social workers is at best incomplete. (See Dingwall, Eekelaar and Murray, 1983.) At the same time, I do not believe that patriarchy has ended in the way that Donzelot seems to suggest. On the contrary, I believe that patriarchal ideas and structures permeate the social sector identified by Donzelot, and that an examination of women's ambivalent relationship with social work will highlight this.

Feminism and familialism in the vigilance discourse

Feminism and familialism were not discrete discourses within the vigilance movement. On the contrary, it was feminism which promoted familialism, and did so in the name of women's rights.

As I have described in Chapter 2, the vigilance movement contained within in a host of assumptions and attitudes towards men, women and children, and specifically, towards correct sexual behaviour. Vigilance and purity campaigners wanted to re-frame sexual mores - to raise men's sexual and moral behaviour to that of women's; and to protect women and children from the unwanted sexual attention of men. This was a very positive, liberating message for women and children - that they should be "free from all uninvited touch of man."[7] At the same time, it was a discourse which placed women on a pedestal of moral superiority, and which defined women and children as passive, helpless creatures who required rescuing and protection.

The family played a key role in vigilance policy and practice. Parents referred their wayward offspring to the NVA; children who ran away from home were taken home as a first option, especially when their parents were considered to be "respectable"; NVA staff addressed countless mothers' meetings advising them how to raise their children to be good, decent adults. They were not alone in doing this. During the 1920s and 1930s there was an explosion in new social/ educational groups which promulgated ideas about the value of motherhood and the correct way to bring up children.

For those young women whose families were unable to care for them, or whose families were deemed to be undesirable and "bad influences", the vigilance solution was re-training in a residential institution (Magdalene asylum or training hostel) to prepare them to take their place in another family setting - as domestic servants in a middle class household. Live-in "situations" in private homes were thought to be good placements for young women because their movements might be monitored and they would learn skills which would be useful to them in their future lives as wives and mothers. Of course, in reality, many women were more at risk of sexual exploitation as servants in middle class families than they had been in their own perhaps chaotic, poor working class families. Rescue homes were found to have a very high percentage of women who had been living as domestic servants. (See J.R. and D.J. Walkowitz, 1974.)

117

Some women were found lodgings and jobs which were not live-in posts. But there was a preference for jobs in hospitals and shops rather than in factories or on farms, which were seen as potential hot-beds of vice and sin. (The jute mills in Dundee came in for special attention in the 1930s, when the NVA in Edinburgh spreads its net to include Dundee, Forfar and Perth.)

The vigilance discourse was, in essence, deeply conservative, aimed at imposing middle class standards of child rearing and "decency" on working class families. Real structural, economic issues to do with poverty and deprivation were viewed as personal failings, to be solved through individualised methods. Yet many of the vigilance protagonists were self-avowed radicals and feminists, fighting for women's rights to education, employment and the vote. Others may not have called themselves feminists, but they devoted their lives to furthering the cause of women.

An examination of NVA committee members in Edinburgh in the vigilance period throws up a number of famous names from the early feminist movement - women doctors instrumental in campaigning for medical provision for women (Dr. Elsie Ingles, Dr Isabel Venters), women teachers, and most influentially, the President of the NVA (Eastern Division) from 1912 to 1930 was Lady Frances Balfour, executive committee member of the National Union of Women's Suffrage Societies.

Lady Frances Balfour's life (1858-1930) gives us an indication of the kind of feminism which she supported. Frances Balfour was a constitutionalist feminist who relied on political lobbying, especially in gaining the support of the Liberal Party, to achieve her ends. She stood apart from the more radical, disruptive tactics of the Pankhursts, and likewise was wary of the demands of socialist feminists. She saw the suffrage movement and the vote for women as a way of unlocking doors for women, not as the first step on the road towards righting women's wrongs.[8] In addition to her suffrage work and support for the vigilance cause, she was involved in a wide variety of other campaigns including Irish home rule, free trade, employment rights for women (for example, the rights of barmaids when the temperance lobby tried to prevent women from working in bars), and campaigns for equal divorce rights and improved custody rights for mothers.

Donzelot (1980) offers an explanation for what may seem like a contradiction between feminism and familialism within the vigilance discourse. He suggests that middle class women in the nineteenth century formed an alliance with doctors and hygienists which enabled them to enter working class homes and teach working class women how to be better wives and mothers. While middle class women were expected to bring up their children in an atmosphere of relative freedom and openness, working class women were encouraged to be responsible for the control of movement not just of their children, but also their husbands. In other words, the middle class sought to impose different values on the working class - values which were related to their idea of what was appropriate behaviour for working class people. Therefore the independence of movement, and release from child care responsibilities which feminist philanthropists sought for themselves would in no way have been a consideration for the working class women with whom they were working.

The vigilance period serves to remind us that women's oppression is not straightforward. The women who played a key role in the agency in its early years were undoubtedly discriminated against on the basis of their gender, through the sexual double standard, as well as through a lack of rights over children, property, employment and the vote. They worked hard to reduce some of this discrimination, while not challenging patriarchy in its wider sense. The women who were clients of the agency found their behaviour regulated and controlled in a previously unheard of way, by a group made up primarily of middle class women.

There is another important point here. A prominent theme in the radical social work literature of the 1970s argued that social work was "in crisis". Social workers were described as finding it increasingly difficult to reconcile the contradictory care and control aspects of their jobs. Increasing convergence between the two was said to be confronting social workers with "irreconcilable objectives", and contributing to the sense of crisis. (Satyamurti, 1979, p. 92.) The vigilance period illustrates that care and control have never been "institutionally separate" in the way in which Satyamurti envisages. There was little distinction to be made between the "caring" philanthropic Magdalene asylums and the "controlling" statutory Lock Hospitals; on the contrary, the regimes in both were very similar. (Mahood, 1990.) Social work has always controlled its clients through a complex mix of reward and punishment, supervision and support, privilege and imposition. This is the means through which it has achieved "corrective training"; the way in which "disciplinary power" in society has been exercised. (Foucault, 1977.)

Feminism and familialism post Second World War

If feminism and familialism went hand in hand during the vigilance period, the same cannot be said of the period after the Second World War. Riley (1988) suggests that feminism became unpopular in 1945, just as it had done in 1918. She identifies that "sex-consciousness" and "sex-antagonism" became deeply pejorative terms, the very antithesis of the comradeship and consensus which everyone wanted to be striving for.

My interviews with staff and committee members who had been young adults during the Second World War confirm Riley's perception.[9] Only one respondent described herself as a feminist. All the others expressed disapproval of the feminism of the Women's Liberation Movement, and expressed concern about a current feminism which they perceived to be "anti-men." The impact of the Second World War seems to have been central to reaching this position. Respondents described to me what an "eye opener" their war time experiences had been. They had come from sheltered, middle class backgrounds and found themselves thrown into an environment working alongside men and women from very different class and social backgrounds. They were officers in the army, in the WRAF, and even in military intelligence. One respondent claimed that for her generation of young women, life would never be the same again:-

> It opened up a whole different attitude to life, and we hadn't had anything behind us to lead us to that point. We were caught in a little time-capsule, which resulted in us having more open minds .... we had learnt a lot between 1940 and 1945.[10]

For this respondent, and for all the women whom I interviewed, there was a sense of purposefulness after the war. A new society had to be built, one in which men and women would take better care of one another, in which class and gender conflicts would be lessened, and children would never again have to undergo the awfulness of wartime neglect and deprivation.

There has been much debate within feminists about the loss of the feminist cause in the light of the building of the welfare state after the Second World War. Some argue that feminism virtually disappeared at this time, as women were "highjacked" by familial ideology and reformism. (Wilson, 1983.) Others claim that feminism did not disappear, and instead went on to have a strong presence within the Labour movement and within socialist politics. Taylor (1983) argues that the "woman question" has been a consistent, periodic feature in socialist politics. Feminists struggled to get welfare provision which would be supportive and helpful to women and which would meet real needs, though this did not imply that there was agreement about how to achieve this. Vera Brittain (1953) expressed some of the hopefulness and idealism of the welfare state:-

> ... in it women have become ends in themselves and not merely means to the ends of men. The welfare state has been both cause and consequence of the second great change by which women have moved

... from rivalry with men to a new recognition of their unique value as women. (Brittain, 1953.)

My examination of Family Care's history leads me to argue that feminism did indeed take on new forms after the Second World War, and that one of the principal ways we can see it being worked out is in the drive to professionalise "women's work" - teaching, nursing, health visiting, and of course, social work.

After the Second World War a group of predominantly women fought to improve working conditions, status and career opportunities within social work. It was here that the aspirations of women might be realised - aspirations to be allowed to carry out useful work, paid or unpaid; to achieve the status and recognition in their working lives that they expected to receive in their home lives; to work alongside male professionals, recognising their unique task as social workers. (See Chapter 4.)

There was a central paradox in the professionalisation of social work, however. In the movement to upgrade their profession, women actively undermined their own position. They did this in two ways, first by seeking to attract more men into the profession, and second by playing down the "feminine" qualities previously considered fundamental to social work. (See Younghusband, 1947.) Social work practitioners and theoreticians (women and men) fought to move social work away from its old image of a "lady bountiful" kind of service which relied for its knowledge and skills on female intuition and motherly love. Instead, social work became more rational, more scientific, more administrative - more "masculine". (Chafetz, 1972.)

This shift inevitably strengthened the position of men within social work. Social work teaching institutions (universities and colleges) which were already heavily biased towards male academics appointed disproportionately high numbers of men to the newly created teaching posts. Later, as welfare services and social work departments grew in size, and social work organisation became more bureaucratic, managerial and administrative, again more men were appointed to the new management posts. (Howe, 1986.) This process has been described as a "defeminisation of social work." (Kravetz, 1976.)

The professionalisation of social work brought gains and losses for women. While men in social work undoubtedly benefited from the process of professionalisation, social work's professionalisation also enabled women to "create careers and personal lives that were powerful, liberating and autonomous." (Chambers, 1986.) At first these opportunities were restricted to upper and middle class women, who could pay for training, or work in pioneering settings for little and sometimes no wages. Later as grants were introduced for social work training, a much wider cross section of women have benefited from access to a career in professional social work. For those women at the bottom of the occupational ladder - the home helps, care assistants and social work assistants - the professionalisation and growth of social work services have offered a range of paid jobs which in the past would not have been waged. (Land, 1991.) But the wages and working conditions attached to these jobs have been anything but "liberating and autonomous."

While feminist energies were channelled into socialist politics and professional development, social work itself was transformed after the Second World War. There was a new awareness of children as separate beings with their own rights and needs separate from those of their parents. There was also a general desire (expressed to me by all respondents who have lived through the war) that something had to be done to safeguard the next generation - that the children of the nation mattered. New statutory and voluntary services grew up in response to this new recognition of "the needs of children". (See Chapter 4.)

But what of evidence of familial ideology on social work? I believe that there was no single, all-pervasive familial ideology at work in the years following the Second World War. Instead what we see is a mixture of discourses and practical exigencies which continued to contribute to the formation of the social work task, and as a result, different kinds of "family" being supported by social workers.

The psycho-analytic approach which came to dominate child care courses and progressive social work settings illustrated a fixed set of gendered and familial ideas. Here we can see particular conceptions about the differences between men and women (as being innate, instinctive differences which were then developed by social circumstances); and about nuclear families with a sexual division of labour (as being the most secure and most healthy upbringing for children); and about heterosexuality as being the desired norm; Freudian notions of Oedipus Complex and male/female identification are important here. (See Barrett and McIntosh, 1982.)

However, although psy experts and social work commentators agreed that wherever possible families provided the best living arrangement for children, there was no necessary agreement about what kind of family best met children's needs. Winnicottt (1944 and 1957) did not devote his energies to analysing *ideal* parenting. He studied "good enough" parenting, and within this broad term he accepted that differences were possible. Likewise, although Bowlby (1941 and 1953) was critical of poor residential care, he did not outlaw *all* residential care. (See also Burlingham and Freud, 1944.)

What I am suggesting here is that "post war familialism" was never as pure a discourse as some feminist critics (such as Wilson, 1977) have presented. Not only that, familial discourse had roots which were much older than the post war period, as the vigilance story illustrates. What we see happening in social work after the war is convergence and competition between older ideas and practices and new ideas about the family, in the context of the given historical moment, in this case, the aftermath of the Second World War.

Adoption practice highlights most clearly a stereotypical familial model. Babies were placed for adoption in nuclear families which lived up to expectations of a sexual division of labour, with husband in the role of bread-winner, and wife choosing to leave work and become a full time housewife and mother. There was no question of wives continuing to work, or of unusual family or marital relationships. Jane Rowe's (1966) manual on adoption evidences this clearly. Here she warns against women "who take too great an interest in their careers and men who drink to excess". (p. 164.) If different patterns of family life did exist, we know nothing about them because prospective adopters were careful not to disclose this to their social workers. Quite simply, all the prospective adopters presented themselves as conventional nuclear families, and many of the women had already given up work in anticipation of motherhood.[11]

But there was another unspoken assumption which grounded adoption in familial ideas at this time. Adoption practice betrayed older notions of environmentalism - the idea that the environment was somehow contagious, and that children needed to be "saved" from the dangerousness of their natural origins. (The later concept of the "cycle of deprivation" proposed by Keith Joseph also illustrates this way of thinking.) In the nineteenth century, the response to fears engendered by environmentalist ideas led to the "rescue" of children from their slums and depravity (as Dr Barnardo did in London) and their transportation to new homes, often as far away as North America and Australia. Closer to home, we can see the policy at work in Edinburgh in the 1940s and 1950s as children who were taken into care were placed with foster parents in remote Highland crofts.[12] Adoption was not, therefore, even at this time, only about placing children in the "happy families" of the 1950s advertisements. It was about giving them a new life, one which was far removed from the disadvantages of their birth.

Casework practice in this agency illustrates social work's support for a non-conventional, non-stereotypical family patterns. The job of caseworkers in the Guild of Service from the 1950s right up to the 1990s was to work with "unmarried mothers" - to provide practical and emotional support to women with illegitimate babies. In the early days of the agency, this support included finding work and accommodation for the mother and child, and pursuing the father to contribute maintenance payments. After the Second

World War, a range of services for unmarried mothers were developed, including casework, residential care, and adoption.

There are two rather different principles operating in the casework with women who chose to keep their babies, neither of which owes its allegiance to post war familial ideology. The first relates to individuation ("individual client self-determination"), that is, respecting the client's right to make her own decision, and supporting her in that decision. (See British Association of Social Workers Principles of Social Work Practice.)[13] The second relates to the idea that children are best brought up in their biological families, even when these families do not match the nuclear family norm. Social work (at least since the Children Act of 1948) has routinely given support to chaotic, disorganised, potentially damaging families. The notion of preventing the break-up of families has been a very potent one. Holman (1988) identifies the Social Work (Scotland) Act of 1968 with its emphasis on "social welfare for all" as the high point in the acceptance of the idea of prevention.

The picture which emerges, therefore, is not a straightforward one of social work oppressing women, or of only one set of ideas influencing the social work task with families. Instead, there has been a constant process of negotiation in daily social work practice.

Feminism and familialism from the 1970s to the 1990s

From the 1970s onwards there has been another struggle to define the relationship between women and the social work task.

On the one hand, social work has been characterised by an increasingly managerial, technical style of operation, which has relied on ever tighter systems and regulations for its implementation. Commentators have pointed out that organisational development over the past twenty years, particularly in the statutory sector but also witnessed in voluntary agencies, has been heading towards a "masculinisation" of the service. Managerial control and bureaucratic intervention have supplemented concerns about quality of service and professional values. (Dominelli and McLeod, 1989, pp. 139-140.) Institutional sexism is such that there is a vertical and horizontal division of labour in social work, with men predominating at the top, and women at the bottom of the occupational ladder. (See Dale and Foster, 1986; Howe, 1986.)

At the same time however, a new feminist discourse in social work has emerged, one which has been articulated in many different areas inside and outside social work, challenging traditional social work knowledge, values and skills/models of intervention.

It was with the appointment of openly feminist social workers (one of whom was me) at the end of the 1970s and into the early 1980s that a new feminist discourse began to struggle for attention in the life of this agency (ironically now under its new title of Family Care.[14]) Work with unmarried mothers and single parents began to have quite a different flavour. The language changed from "single parents" to "women", and a group work project started in the Muirhouse council housing scheme was targeted at all women, not simply single parents or mothers. As the targets of intervention changed, so did the styles and methods of working. The individual client-social worker/professional social work relationship was replaced by a more open system in which women were encouraged to support one another, and in which participation was grounded in an acceptance of women's shared experiences.

By 1985 the Muirhouse group successfully convinced the agency and the Housing Department to give it the use of a council flat for a new women's centre, and No.20 was born. No.20 proudly described itself as the first community based women's centre in Scotland. Its early aims and objectives were:-

> to provide a supportive environment for women to meet in, space for them to develop as individuals, an opportunity to share in decision-making and to take on responsibilities in the project.[15]

No.20 reflected all of the idealism and excitement of the new feminist social work movement. For those of us who were part of it, it was an opportunity to bring our private and professional selves together - to put feminism principles into practice in our work for the first time. Articles were written for social work journals, social work students competed to get placements at No.20, and working class women came together to help one another and to join groups on everything from domestic violence to adult basic education.

But No.20 had to change, and this reflects a central dilemma in social work's relationship with women. When No.20 began, a crèche worker was employed to look after the children while the women took part in different groups. This was in recognition of the fact that the groups were important. They were regarded as comparable with work, and women should be enabled to concentrate in the groups without interference of noisy toddlers. Of course we hoped that the crèche would be a stimulating and enjoyable experience for the children, but this was not its prime objective.

As No.20 developed, so the work with the children came to have a much more significant function. We were faced with the reality that many of the children coming to No.20 were being neglected and abused by society, by care-givers (partners and fathers), and, most difficult for us to confront, by their mothers - at times, emotionally, verbally and physically. Understanding the structural origins of child abuse (in the parents' personal histories and in the patriarchal, capitalist society we live in) did nothing to diminish the hurt and pain experienced by some of these children. In two specific cases, steps had to be taken to remove children into alternative care. For the rest of the children, the focus shifted from keeping them quiet, to setting out to repair some of the damage done to them by poverty and neglect. The children's playroom was moved into a bigger room, and a play worker replaced the sessional crèche worker. No.20 still exists today, and is described in current Family Care literature as a "women and children's centre".

I have told this story in detail because it highlights one of the big questions facing social work today, that is, is it ever possible to carry out feminist social work? Dominelli and McLeod (1989) argue that the development of feminist practice, even in statutory social work, is essential. (p. 126.) Sue Wise (1990) takes a more cautious stance. Herself a feminist, she identifies that the needs of women and children are frequently in conflict with one another, and that this necessarily means at times acting for children against the wishes of women. My experience as a social worker accords with this perception. Feminist social work practice becomes, then, not a rejection of social control in social work, but an acceptance of it. Wise goes on to argue that this leads to the posing of different kinds of questions, about what feminism can tell us about "acceptable standards" of care, who should decide what these are, and how they should be imposed. (p. 248.) (This links back to Chapter 2, where I argue that care and control are legitimate tasks within social work.)

The feminist discourse which grounded the social work at No.20 did not revolutionise all other agency practice in Family Care. At the same time as No.20 opened, the agency began an adoption counselling service for all those involved in the different aspects of the adoption process (adopters, adoptees and birth parents.) The Adoption Counselling Centre worked from a traditional professional social work model. There was no suggestion here of insights from new feminist counselling methods being employed (see Chaplin, 1988), or of a special interest in gender issues. On the contrary, there was some hostility (more latent than expressed) between the Adoption Counselling Centre social workers who rejected feminist approaches and the single parent families' social workers who described themselves as feminists and chose to work mainly with women.[16]

So how could one agency be pulling in two such different directions at the same time? The answer lies partly in the background and personal orientation of the social workers employed at this time. Some of us had a history of involvement in the Women's Liberation Movement and in feminist activities; others did not. But this is too simplistic an answer. More importantly, the agency, in common with most social work agencies has never described itself as a feminist agency, and has never taken on board in any overall sense issues of women's oppression. Its alignment has been to other professional social work agencies, not women's organisations. (See Hudson, 1989, p. 76)

In the 1980s alongside feminist and professional social work concepts, a new discourse appeared in the agency, built on acceptance of the tenets of American management theory. The language was masculine, with a lot of attention given to targets and strategies, to efficiency, cost effectiveness and workload management. One business-man committee member whom I interviewed talked to me about the merits of good "man-management" (all but one of the staff were women) and argued that the agency needed a manager as director, not a social worker: someone who would be able to stand back from the needs of the clients (from the "feelings") and make the "hard decisions" which were necessary.[17] A new Director has now shifted the pendulum back in favour of "social work values" as opposed to "management-speak",[18] but this is in marked contrast to the style which today predominates in the outside world of social work, as seen in social work training and government publications on Community Care and Criminal Justice.

Summary

My conclusions lead me back to the beginning of the chapter, to the assertion that although discourses which define women and the family have been enormously influential in determining the nature of the social work task, their impact has not been static, one dimensional or unchallenged. Instead, feminist and familialist strands have existed side by side and in contradiction with one another, (and with other discourses in social work) throughout the history of social work this century. Therefore we have seen that although the welfare state in general, and social work in particular, is sexist, it is not *only* sexist. Maintaining sexism in society is not the sole condition of its existence. Instead, the development of social work has brought with it the possibility of career advancement and self actualisation for many women who have chosen to work in the field; and the possibility of support and protection for vulnerable groups in society, who are predominantly women and children.

This support and protection has, of course, been viewed negatively as well as positively. Wilson (1977) perceives preventive social work as a form of social containment which seeks to maintain women's subordination in the family. My own approach is a more pragmatic one. I have no doubt that social work is structured to be a form of social control, and that social workers do have power over the families with whom they are working. Yet I believe nevertheless that a caring kind of social work is possible, even within the tight limitations of statutory social work. I believe also that the contradictions for women within the social work discourse echo much wider contradictions for women in society as a whole. Social control has positive as well as negative aspects, giving social workers permission to intervene on behalf of abused children, and at the same time affording the state greater surveillance of family life. In one of his last interviews, Foucault argued that no discourse is inherently liberating or oppressive - "not everything is bad, but everything is dangerous."(Foucault, 1984, in Bernauer and Rasmussen, 1988.) The story of the NVA shows us how a discourse which set out to be progressive and pro-feminist can at the same time promote and justify behaviour which is both reactionary and suppressive; just as social work today has the capacity to be supportive as well as punitive.

My final statement is an optimistic one. If discourse is partial in its effect, challenged as it is by other discourses and by practical circumstances, then resistance and change are possible. It is therefore up to us women engaged in creating the social work task today to seek to build a social work policy and practice which is gender-aware in its theory and non-oppressive in its method.

Notes

1. Interview with Janet Lusk, 25-05-90.
2. Interview, 13-02-91.
3. Quotation by Marion Phillips, executive member of the women's section of the Labour Party in the 1920s, from D. Riley (1988).
4. "The Work of Women as Poor Law Guardians", *Westminster Review*, Vol. 123, 1885, from Hollis (1979).
5. Interviews, 30-05-90, 22-10-90.
6. Donzelot's work has been criticised not only because it is obtuse and difficult to read, but because he betrays some very sexist and anti-feminist writing. It has been suggested that Donzelot mourns the loss of the patriarchal family, and blames women for this process. (See Barrett and McIntosh, 1982, pp. 95-105; Bennet et al, 1981; Hirst, 1981.) Donzelot would argue that his work is purely descriptive, and that he does not take sides on this question.
7. E. Ethelmer (pen-name of Elizabeth Wolstenholme-Elmy) (1893),

Continued

Woman Free, Women's Emancipation Union, Congleton, p. 20.

8.   From Lady Frances Balfour's memoirs:- Lady F. Balfour (1930), *Me Obliviscaris*, Hodder and Stoughton, London.   Also entry on Balfour in Banks (1985) pp. 10-12.

9.   Interviews with six staff members and six committee members who joined the agency after the war and into the 1950s.

10.   Interview, 23-05-91.

11.   Couples were turned down for other reasons - low anticipated life expectancy; mental health problems; poor marital relationship.   Case records, 1950s and 1960s.

12.   Interview, 09-04-91.

13.   BASW Principles of Social Work Practice include:-"Respect for clients as individuals and safeguarding their participation in decisions and defining services." BASW, Birmingham.

14.   The new name was chosen as sufficiently all-encompassing that it would not only cover the present work of the agency, but leave room for possible developments in the future. It was also felt to be non-contentious, and likely to invoke the sympathy of the general public when it came to raising funds.   Interview with Janet Lusk, 25-05-90.

15.   No. 20 Aims and Objectives, internal paper 1985.

16.   My experience and interviews with social workers from both sides of the debate confirm this point.

17.   Interview, 20-06-91.

18.   Interview with Jennifer Speirs, 02-07-91.

7 Voluntary social work –
A moving frontier

Introduction

When Lord Beveridge in 1949 applauded "the perpetually moving frontier of voluntary action",[1] he was drawing attention to what he saw as an essential quality of voluntary agencies, that is, their capacity to "trail-blaze" - to continually initiate new services which then become part of the social fabric. In this chapter I will argue that the voluntary sector has indeed been a moving frontier, though not always for the reasons anticipated by Beveridge. I will argue that the voluntary sector has been in a constant state of struggle, from its early battles to retain its position as a primary service provider and initiator, to its present day dilemmas as it tries to hold onto its independence and its raison d'être in the world of the "new realities". (Drucker, 1989.) This may seem a surprising stance to take, given the government's commitment to "handing services back" to non-statutory agencies. However, I will argue that in the current climate of short term contracts and packages of care, voluntary organisations risk losing their independence, their freedom and their rationale, as they become little more than cheaper substitutes of governmental enterprise.

The current uncertainties surrounding the voluntary sector must be seen as part of an ongoing debate about the relationship between the individual and the state. The provision of social welfare has always been a battleground; an arena of conflict and contestation in which competing groups and ideologies have fought for prominence and legitimacy. The question of who provides welfare, and what welfare is provided, has never been a neutral subject, nor an area of total consensus. On the contrary, the whole history of welfare is characterised by ideological debate about who should and should not provide welfare.

The complexities do not end here, however. The welfare state is not only a set of ideas about how society should be organised. It is also a set of practices - real, practical solutions must be found to pressing social and economic problems. Policies therefore bear witness to compromises and practical exigencies as much as to pure ideology. Economic and political imperatives may be as important as altruism and aspirations for redistribution. (Thane, 1982, p. 294.)

Four sectors have traditionally been involved in welfare provision - commercial and informal sectors, as well as voluntary and statutory sectors. In this chapter, I will address the changing position of the voluntary sector, and in particular, Family Care, as it has fought to retain its status and its usefulness, in the face of an ever increasing and more powerful statutory sector.

Voluntary versus statutory social welfare discourses

Voluntary social welfare discourse reached a peak in the nineteenth century in the administration of the Poor Law and the Charity Organisation Society. Responsibility for welfare provision was placed firmly on individuals, families and communities, because it was assumed that most people's needs were best met by relying on their own resources, or on those of the community, particularly local charitable and voluntary associations. The emphasis in welfare was on self help and the cultivation of independence, with the aim that the claimant would be better able to cope with his/her problems in the future. The role of the state was to care for "the residue" of "undeserving poor", those unable to help themselves. Statutory aid was always viewed as potentially dangerous because it took something away from the recipient and might result in dependence and pauperisation.

This has been called the "parallel bars" concept of voluntary and statutory welfare. Each was regarded as a separate and mutually exclusive sector, with the voluntary sector providing for the bulk of social care needs. This was the view which dominated the Majority Report to the Poor Law Commission.[2]

In contrast, statutory welfare ideology, which came to the fore in the post-Second World War "Butskellite consensus" was governed by a belief in the duty of the state to provide a basic minimum standard of living for all its citizens, though of course the level at which this was set remained open to debate. There was a strongly egalitarian, universalising strand in this discourse, an assumption that there should be no shame in claiming welfare or in seeing a social worker. Social welfare was a right to be claimed if and when it is needed by all citizens. There was also a heavily centralist component in the thinking and in the legislation - a belief in central planning and a concern to do away with individualistic, ad hoc, localised solutions. The role of voluntary welfare became identified as that of a supplementer of statutory services, doing things which statutory services were not already doing, and an initiator of new services.

This "extension ladder" theory was first proposed by the Webbs in the Minority Report to the Poor Law Commission, and became the generally accepted position from the 1940s up until the 1970s, as evidenced in the Children Act of 1948, the Children and Young Persons' Act of 1963, and the Social Work (Scotland) Act of 1968.

It was the 1970s - a time of unprecedented expansion in statutory welfare services - which was also the time when the fragile consensus on the welfare state finally collapsed. Voices from left and right of the political spectrum rose to attack both the ideological foundations and the practical achievements of the welfare state and statutory social welfare. Those on the left condemned the welfare state for its non-participatory, alienating structures, and its ineffectiveness at meeting real social need. Those on the right attacked its dependency-inducing, lacking-in-choice systems, and its inefficiency. Norman Fowler summed this up in 1984, arguing:- "The state has not, cannot, and should not monopolise the personal social services."[3]

But the assault on the legitimacy of the welfare state and statutory services was not a new phenomenon. Even at the time of the inception of the welfare state, concerns had continued to be expressed about the rightness and feasibility of universal state provision. (Hayek, 1944.) These concerns were enshrined in the actual mechanics of the welfare benefit system as it was translated into practice, and evidenced in statutory welfare's persistent use of the contributory principle and in the various "means tests" surrounding welfare benefits. Marsh (1970) suggests that the emphasis on universality in state welfare services has obscured the fact that benefits have *always* been limited to "persons having specified needs in times of specified contingencies". (pp. 6-7.) The welfare state never did assume responsibility for all social needs, and instead continued to use the voluntary sector to carry out work on its behalf.

Two related sets of ideas have emerged, promoting a new way forward in the debate around statutory and voluntary welfare. The first centres on the notion of decentralisation, often expressed in terms of "community social work", or "patch", and reflected in the Barclay Report of 1982. The Barclay Report stressed the complimentarity of the statutory and voluntary sectors. Each should compensate for weaknesses in the other, by working together to plan a "mutually reinforcing" partnership. This would be achieved by the personal social services developing much closer links with informal networks

132

of local citizens and with voluntary organisations in the planning and delivery of services, that is, in "community social work". (See Hadley and Hatch, 1981.)

The second set of ideas develops the concept of "welfare pluralism", a term which originated in the United States (see Berger and Neuhaus, 1977), but which has been taken up by supporters of the voluntary sector in Britain. Welfare pluralism was first advanced in Britain in the *Wolfenden Report* of 1978, and developed in Francis Gladstone's polemic *Voluntary Action in a Changing World,* (Gladstone, 1979). Here he lays out the voluntary sector's case for "gradualist welfare pluralism." He argues for the gradual substitution of statutory services by voluntary action, the role of the state becoming that of resource allocator and service monitor rather than service provider. He upholds the potential for voluntary action to offer a way out of the present difficulties in the welfare state, claiming its superior ability to provide services on the grounds of its greater adaptability; its cost effectiveness; its enhanced level of participation; and its more co-ordinated approach towards welfare provision within the context of neighbourhoods.

It was welfare pluralism which succeeded in capturing the imagination of policy makers and legislators. The idea of welfare pluralism is central to the *Griffiths Report* of 1988 and at the heart of current community care legislation. (*Caring for People,* 1989; NHS and Community Care Act, 1990.) Here a clear split is delineated between purchaser and provider roles, with the statutory sector given the task of purchasing services in the market place of care on behalf of clients. The expectation that the statutory sector should carry a primary responsibility for welfare provision has gone. In its place, statutory, voluntary, "not for profit" and commercial agencies are all expected to compete with one another for contracts to provide individualised packages of care.

Brenton (1985) is critical of the mystique surrounding welfare pluralism. She doubts whether voluntary agencies are essentially more innovative, more participatory, and more cost effective than statutory agencies, and suggests that these are at the most "potential attributes" of the voluntary sector. More fundamentally, Brenton asks how much of a mixed economy of welfare is *really* being advanced, and how far instead this represents a retreat for the state. (See also Beresford and Croft, 1984.) Brenton draws attention to the lack of an analysis of power or class in the pluralist approach:-

> There is no space here for a structural view of society as the arena of conflicts between the interests of institutionalised and concentrated power and the powerless, between a class which keeps an iron grip on essential economic and political resources and a class which ... is

133

confined to a permanently unequal position in society. (Brenton, 1985, p. 222.)

This brings me back to my initial statement, that the relationship between voluntary and statutory social welfare is invariably problematic and always political. There is no consensus about how welfare should be provided and by whom. The social work task is therefore an arena of intense struggle and strategic manoeuvring, as my historical case study will illustrate.

Definitions - voluntary and statutory agencies

The question of what constitutes voluntary social work is not without controversy, and different writers have adopted different meanings and emphases. (For a range of views, see Brenton, 1985; Hatch, 1980; Johnson, 1981; Murray, 1969; Rooff, 1957; Wolfenden, 1978.)

At a general level, voluntary social work agencies may be assumed to be organisations which rely on voluntary effort, paid for by voluntary funds, to provide services for particular identified groups or social problems. But in reality, the picture is far more complicated. Brenton (1985) argues that the definition of a voluntary organisation is "essentially a statement of an ideal type based on a constellation of features some of which or all of which may be conformed to by voluntary organisations in practice." (p. 9.)

A brief examination of the range of voluntary organisations operating in Scotland today accords with Brenton's assessment. Some voluntary organisations rely almost totally on volunteer input (for example, Citizen's Advice Scotland, and many other self help groups) while others make no use of volunteers at all (for example, Edinburgh Family Service Unit.) Similarly, while some voluntary agencies do a substantial amount of fund raising (for example, Barnardo's), others depend on 100 per cent government financial support (for example, the Volunteer Centre.)

Some voluntary organisations provide services, often paid for to a substantial degree by local authorities or central government (again, like the Family Service Unit or Family Care). Others concentrate on co-ordination and/or pressure group activities (for example, Edinburgh Voluntary Organisations' Council.) And many organisations represent a hybrid of all of these, providing some services and some advocacy functions, some mutual aid and some professional support, paid for by a patchwork of independent fund raising and local and central government backing (for example, Scottish Council for Single Parents.)

To further complicate matters, some voluntary agencies are small, locally based organisations (including local tenants' associations) while others operate at a national level, such as Age Concern or Childline (though again, these national organisations are likely to have local committees with only tenuous links with their national headquarters.)

If voluntary organisations are difficult to pin down, then statutory organisations are equally so. Private fund raising lies at the core of much statutory health and welfare service provision (for example, the huge sums raised by cancer and AIDS charities for the National Health Service, or the "Sick Kids Appeal" in Edinburgh which raised £11.5 million for a new wing at the Royal Hospital for Sick Children.) And voluntary organisations have not been the sole users of volunteers either. Health service and social work departments have made considerable use of unpaid workers in the provision and maintenance of a range of services to clients (for example, meals on wheels, hospital libraries and canteens, and befriending services.)

Kramer (1981) in his analysis of voluntary agencies in the welfare state identifies four key functions carried out by voluntary agencies. They are expected to be "innovative and flexible, to protect particularistic interests, to promote voluntary citizen participation, and to meet needs not met by government". (p. 4.) This provides a useful framework and one which I will adopt to study the changes in the relationship between voluntary and statutory welfare as we see them being worked out at Family Care.

Before going onto an in-depth examination of Family Care's development, it is important to re-state that Family Care is an example of a particular kind of voluntary organisation, and cannot be seen as representative of *all* voluntary activity. Family Care is a medium sized, Edinburgh based professional social work agency which has sought to be in the vanguard of the establishment of good social work practice in Britain. Staff are paid and professionally qualified. Finance comes from a range of sources - donations, fund raising, and local and central government. Volunteer activity is limited to two proscribed areas, fund raising and befriending.

While Family Care has found it increasingly difficult to maintain its position in the social work world, this does not imply that all voluntary agencies have experienced the same difficulties. From the 1970s onwards, thousands of new voluntary agencies have grown up, many of them in the value guardian and improver roles. Many of them also provide services to their members; services which are often qualitatively different to those provided by statutory agencies. Some of these new agencies are small, locally based self help groups or single issue campaigns. But new national voluntary organisations have also emerged since 1970. In 1994, the gross annual income to voluntary organisations in Scotland was £2 billion.[4]

The vanguard role

Voluntary organisations are expected to innovate, to pioneer, to experiment and to demonstrate programmes, some of which may later be adopted by statutory authorities. (Kramer, 1981, pp. 173-192.) This "trail-blazing" notion permeates all government reports and legislation on voluntary organisations, and most writing from within and outwith the voluntary sector. From the *Beveridge Report* of 1942 to the *Barclay Report* of 1982 and a plethora of recent literature around welfare pluralism, the mythology has been created and maintained that suggests that voluntary agencies are not only good at pioneering, but are somehow in a better position to innovate than statutory agencies.

But is this true? How far does the example of Family Care live up to this ideal? There can be no doubt that in its beginnings, Family Care (then the NVA) was in the vanguard role. The work which the agency chose to carry out, from its campaigning activities to the support services it provided for vulnerable women and children, was not being offered in the same way by any other agency, and certainly not by a statutory agency. With a limited range of organisations in the social welfare field, the agency was free to develop services in which ever direction it chose, and significantly, if and when it was able to raise public funds to begin a new project. (Financial support was always easier to obtain when the target was needy children.)

Edzell Lodge Children's Home in its early years matched the stereotypical pioneering role. It was hailed as the first family group home in Scotland, and provided an example and a demonstration for countless visitors who came to find out about its operation. Likewise the adoption practice established by the agency (now the Guild of Service) in the late 1950s and 1960s was regarded by the agency and by other commentators, as pioneering. (See Younghusband, 1964)

But what of the later stages? Kramer suggests that once an agency has become institutionalised, innovation tends to consist of "small scale, non-controversial, incremental improvements or extensions of conventional social services with relatively few original or novel features." (Kramer, 1981, p. 477.) He continues that to find true innovation from the 1960s onwards, we must look to the new self help groups which grew up spontaneously, not to the older established agencies, which used the opportunity of greater statutory resources to expand, rather than to innovate.

Certainly, the Guild of Service did well out of the increase in financial resources available to both statutory and voluntary agencies in the period after the Social Work (Scotland) Act of 1968. The agency was able to offer salaries and conditions of service broadly comparable with that of the local

136

authority - "a great leap forward," according to the agency's secretary/ treasurer.[5] And it was able to increase its staffing levels too. But the Guild of Service did not use the opportunity to expand at this time, and instead chose to consolidate its existing services. When invited to set up branches in Dundee and Aberdeen the Guild of Service refused to do so, on the grounds that local identity and excellence in practice were more important than expansion to new centres of population. Instead, the Guild of Service pioneered two new ventures in the early 1970s. In 1973, the agency became host and manager to the newly formed South East Scotland Resource Centre (SESRC), an adoption consortium made up of all the adoption societies (statutory and voluntary) in the area. SESRC acted as a clearing house for all "hard to place" children, finding adopters for children from within its wide membership. The same year, the Guild of Service piloted a Volunteer Scheme, which recruited, trained and matched volunteer befrienders for single parent families.

While both of these were new and exciting projects, they can also be regarded as incremental rather than trail-blazing. The SESRC was in effect a localised, Scottish version of the London based Adoption Resource Exchange which the Guild of Service had been a member of for a number of years. Translating the London set up to the local situation was a good idea in terms of adoption practice, but it was not a totally original idea.

The volunteers' project arose out of the findings of research into the needs of single mothers sponsored by the Scottish Council for Single Parents (SCSP), and carried out by an ex-Guild of Service social worker. (Hopkinson, 1976.) The research indicated that what most single mothers needed, (apart from more money and better housing), was support from a friend, not a social worker. Volunteers were identified as those most able to provide this supportive friendship to single mothers.

The early 1970s was a time of widespread interest in volunteers and volunteering, highlighted in the *Aves Report* of 1969, and evidenced in the establishment of a host of volunteer initiatives in voluntary and statutory social work settings. The Guild of Service's volunteer scheme, rather than breaking new ground, can be seen as indicative of this general interest in the use of volunteers. (See Chapter 4.)

More recent attempts at innovation have been extremely problematic for the agency, for both financial and practical reasons. In 1982, the agency (now Family Care) introduced three new projects. A play visiting scheme in the Greendykes area of Edinburgh grew out of the work with volunteers; a self help group for women began in another housing scheme, Muirhouse, and arising out of the work with single parents; and an adoption counselling project developed as a response to work already being done by adoption social workers. All of these were initially small scale, incremental projects as Kramer has suggested; and each reflected the idiosyncratic interests and preferences of individual members of staff. There seems to have been no clear sense at this time of the agency taking a policy decision to develop a new area of work. Instead, the agency was pulled in different directions, as staff members struggled to address what they perceived as new unmet needs in their own areas of expertise.

Family Care's involvement in Greendykes ended after three years, because the incoming Family Care Director did not see this work as a priority for the agency.[6] The Muirhouse group expanded to become a full time centre for women and children, more by chance than because of deliberate policy. Funds from the sale of the children's home were used to set up the Muirhouse centre, after plans for a residential Family Centre failed. The adoption counselling project, which was established as a project separate from the agency, moved into Family Care's core work to become the largest activity currently undertaken by the agency. Again, this reflects the failure to get other projects off the ground, as well as the special interest of another new Director in this side of the agency's work.

The whole process of innovation, therefore, is affected not just by professional ideologies or the vision of the agency's director and Executive Committee, it is also a matter of pragmatic reality - of seizing the moment and planning on the basis of what is feasible. But there is another dimension here. Family Care was increasingly dependent on the agreement and approval of its "partners" in the welfare field - the statutory and voluntary agencies with whom it worked and alongside whom it carved out its place in the welfare network.

Family Care's failure to get a new, controversial scheme off the ground highlights the difficulties of innovation in the face of an unsympathetic policy environment. The agency tried without success between 1979 and 1991 to open a new Family Centre - a residential unit with day care facilities for parents and children. The first attempt came via a proposal for a merger with the failing Claremont Park Home for mothers and babies, between 1979 and 1982. But Claremont Park resisted Family Care's approaches. Then when Edzell Lodge Children's Home was forced to close in 1984 (following a policy decision made by the Social Work Department that children should no longer be placed in residential care[7]), Family Care tried again to secure funding to run a residential unit for parents within the Edzell Lodge building. Although consumer research indicated that such a unit was needed, there were concerns about the viability of a unit in a suburban area like Morningside, and in a converted children's home. There were also residual concerns that this unit was an old fashioned idea - that it was a mother and baby home by any other name, and that it perhaps should not be given full support.[8] Funding could not be secured for the proposal, and Edzell Lodge was sold. The agency thereafter put its energies into presenting a joint plan with a voluntary housing association for a unit to be built in the Bingham council housing scheme. Between 1989 and 1991, this project was pursued with both local authority and central government funding bodies without success, and plans were finally shelved in 1991.

Lack of success with the Family Centre illustrates how hard it is for a small voluntary agency to pioneer a project on such a large scale (staffing levels were high), and more importantly, to pioneer a project seen as unfashionable. The agency did have an opportunity when Edzell Lodge closed to "go it alone" - to set up without governmental financial backing, and to prove the project's usefulness in the process. But the stakes were seen as too high. The agency risked losing all its capital and becoming bankrupt if the centre had not been able to quickly become a viable concern.[9]

The idea of training young single mothers for parenthood has been popular again in the recent years. Conservative Party spokesmen and women have rehearsed many of the old arguments about single parents and housing, single parents and promiscuity, single parents and welfare benefits, arguing that there needs to be tighter control over single parents, and particularly over young single mothers. We can see in the Family Centre project the familiar desire to guide and control behaviour and attitudes through surveillance, "normalising judgement" and assessment ("examination"). (See Foucault, 1977.)

There is no doubt that the "contract culture" of the 1990s is going to make it even more difficult for voluntary agencies to experiment with projects which do not have the blessing of local and/or central governmental agencies. When Lothian Region carried out a review of Family Care in 1991, the outcome was that the block grant system disappeared. Instead of giving the agency a lump sum for general services, now cash was tied to designated projects, and specified targets were set for the projects receiving funding. It is a matter of speculation how much scope there will be for the vanguard role in voluntary agencies in the years ahead, as local authorities set standards at the same time as contracting other agencies to provide services on their behalf.

The value guardian role and volunteerism

Kramer (1981) identifies a second traditional quality in the mythology of voluntary agencies, that is, their role as "guards" of a host of social values, including altruism, social integration, democratic collective action, self help, pluralism, humanising and personalising social service. In addition, he states, they are legitimated to preserve the particularistic interests and values of minority groups in society. (Kramer, 1981, pp. 193-211.)

While this may represent the idea of voluntary agencies, practice is often very different. Kramer claims that voluntary agencies are not necessarily participative, democratic organisations which value consumer and volunteer involvement; that volunteerism can be regarded inappropriately as a substitute for paid staff and a way of compensating for deficiencies in the state; and that volunteer growth seems more likely to be found in self help/ advocacy type organisations and in volunteer programmes sponsored by government, than in professionalised, bureaucratic voluntary organisations.

Family Care provides a clear illustration of Kramer's professionalised, bureaucratised voluntary organisation. As I have detailed in Chapter Four, this agency made a deliberate move away from volunteer involvement as part of its professionalisation process from the 1950s to the 1970s. Not only were volunteers removed from direct service provision with clients, they were also gradually distanced from decision making and policy matters. Experts (paediatricians, lawyers, psychologists and psychiatrists) became advisers on individual cases, and the professional social work voice increasingly dominated discussions at committee level. Volunteers were relegated largely to fund raising activities, working in the Thrift Shop and serving at coffee mornings, and playing a peripheral part in agency management and policy making. The volunteer befriending scheme which was initiated in 1973 did not itself challenge or change the agency's overall approach to volunteer involvement. The volunteer scheme owed much greater allegiance to professional social work values than to those of self help or democratic involvement and participation. (See Chapter 4.)

Clients' opportunities for participation in decision making in Family Care have also been limited. Although the agency has made good use of some of its adopters as committee members and chairmen, there has been no opportunity for single parents to contribute to agency policy and practice at executive level. In fact the agency has displayed a marked ambivalence to user involvement in recent years, encouraging users to put pressure on outside funders on the one hand and refusing to act on demands for self management on the other. There have been two instances in recent years when agency clients have been promoted as the voice of the agency - in 1988 when funding for a befriending scheme for young people leaving care (Youth Link) came to an end,[10] and in 1990 when Lothian Region Social Work committee cut its grant aid to Family Care and members of the Muirhouse project (No.20) took to the streets. These were isolated incidents however, and the agency did not take the opportunity to act on and develop user involvement after these events. Just as significant, Family Care has been unable to agree to proposals for local self management for No. 20, much to the disappointment of the women and staff members.[11]

There is little in Family Care's past or present to indicate advocacy or empowerment as identified by welfare pluralists - voluntary organisations being promoted as a means towards "enfranchising thousands of people in this country for whom other opportunities to meet human needs and influence decision making are remote and haphazard." (Hinton and Clyde, 1982, p. 12.) I agree with Kramer that voluntary agencies are not necessarily the value guardians that we might expect or wish them to be. Family Care, by being so tied to the virtues of professionalism, has chosen to underplay the importance of participation and community involvement. While pockets of participation and self help are visible in specific agency projects such as No.20, these have had little impact on the dominant professional discourse of the agency.

The improver role and advocacy

Kramer (1981) notes that apart from their functions as pioneers and value guardians, voluntary agencies are also supposed to serve as "a progressive force for an enlightened and humane social policy." There is, he asserts, both a moral and legal sanction for voluntary agencies "to mediate between the citizen and the state." (Kramer, 1981, pp. 212-232.)

The NVA's primary function was indeed to serve as mediator and improver. As I have described in Chapter Two, the NVA was established in order to fight for tougher legislation on morality, while at the same time to argue that its control remain in voluntary, not state hands. The NVA saw itself as educating both government and people on a wide range of matters to do with public and private sexual behaviour.

When the agency moved away from the vigilance cause towards professional casework, its "improving" energies were directed towards upgrading standards of social work practice in both voluntary and statutory agencies. Much of this work was carried out by the Family Care Director, Janet Lusk, through various groupings and committees on which she exerted a powerful presence (often in the role of chairman), including the Standing Conference of Societies Registered for Adoption, the Scottish Association of Voluntary Child Care Organisations, the Association of Directors of Social Work, and the Houghton Committee into adoption practice. Family Care saw its role at this time as standard bearer and promoter of good, professional social work practice, and Janet Lusk spent more time outwith the agency encouraging and training others than she did within it.[12]

While the agency developed professional practice across Scotland, it no longer spoke publicly on matters connected with sexual behaviour or morality. A number of new specialised pressure groups had entered the field, including the Scottish Council for the Unmarried Mother and her Child (SCUM) in 1942. As SCUM's authority and importance grew, so it was SCUM which began to take the leading role in co-ordinating activities of voluntary organisations working with unmarried mothers; in pressing central government for a better deal for single parents; and in urging local authorities to improve services to enable unmarried mothers to keep their babies. Some of SCUM's work was overtly political, for example its decision to work to close down mother and baby homes in the 1960s.[13] SCUM (later to be renamed Scottish Council for Single Parents) worked closely with the Guild of Service (Family Care), with the broad understanding that one agency would concentrate on professional service development while the other would take the greater share in the more political activities.[14]

The service provider role

Kramer (1981) describes three ways in which voluntary agencies may provide services in the welfare state. They may be primary service providers, doing work for which there is no governmental counterpart. They may complement governmental provision with services which are qualitatively different from those provided by the state. And they may supplement or extend governmental provision with a similar service, at times serving as a substitute for state service. (Kramer, 1981, pp. 232-254.)

Historically we can see the voluntary sector in Scotland occupying different positions at different times. Up until the early 1970s, voluntary agencies were responsible for catering for the bulk of social need not met by the informal sector of family and friends. They were, in effect, the primary service providers. Although legislation from the 1870s onwards had started the process of a shift towards statutory services and statutory control,[15] it was not until after the Social Work (Scotland) Act of 1968 that statutory provision was on a scale likely to usurp the traditional place of voluntary organisations.

Since the 1970s, voluntary agencies have had to find a new role for themselves, largely as supplementary and complementary service providers. As local authorities expanded and gradually took over responsibility for a comprehensive range of primary services, voluntaries have struggled to build a meaningful partnership with local authorities, in the hope that local authorities would continue to fund their complementary and often specialist services.

In more recent years there has been another shift, as central government has passed legislation designed to move statutory agencies out of the role of service provider, and into the role of purchaser and monitor of services provided by other agencies, both voluntary and private. The impact on the voluntary sector has been considerable. Contracts and service agreements are replacing the old system in which local authorities gave grant aid to voluntary agencies. While for some agencies there will be the promise of more cash funding then ever before, it seems likely that opportunities for innovation and experimentation may be reduced. Voluntary agencies are having to look all the more to industry and business for financial support to carry out work which does not come within the restricted priorities set by local or central government. (George, 1994.) At the same time, voluntary agencies are finding themselves increasingly forced to compete against the new "non-statutory" agencies for contracts to deliver services - the new private commercial and "not-for-profit" agencies who have entered the market of care.

Children Act, 1948

We can see the beginnings of a shift in the relationship between the statutory and voluntary agencies engaged in the provision of services for children in the Children Act of 1948. The Children Act had two main purposes - to make new provision for children deprived of a normal home life who had previously been catered for by the Poor Law, and to put into effect the principal recommendations of the Clyde Committee (in Scotland) and the Curtis Committee (in England and Wales). In addition, the Act allowed local authorities to make grants to voluntary child care agencies, and introduced new regulations for monitoring children in residential care and children who were boarded out by voluntary agencies.

This was not statist legislation imposed on a reluctant voluntary sector. On the contrary, representatives from powerful voluntary organisations (including the Guild of Service) were involved in the process of drawing up the legislation. They saw the need for a greater role for the state, and a tightening up and improving of general standards of care for children.

In spite of its universalist aspirations, funding levels were extremely low. Large cities like Edinburgh were serviced by a small staff of one Children's Officer and three assistants, all untrained and unqualified.[16] Jim Johnston, first Director of the new Social Work Department in Glasgow in 1969, described the old child care and welfare departments as "grim":-

> They had to exist, by law. But many of them existed in little more than nominal form, and depended for their effect on tiny numbers of people who rarely had any relevant training. They provided rudimentary services for the old and the handicapped and, in rather greater measure, for deprived children. (Johnston, 1974, p. 17.)

Respondents whom I have interviewed have told me that the Children Act had little or no impact on social work at the Guild of Service. Although more children in general came into care after this time, (Heywood, 1965, p. 161), and there was now some money available to pay for children in voluntary children's homes, the Guild of Service's children's homes were already full. Guild of Service staff therefore experienced the Children Act largely in terms of increased bureaucracy, keeping the Children's Department in touch with movements of children. Caseworkers were in no doubt that their own standards of practice were far in advance of those of the new Departments.[17]

Social Work (Scotland) Act, 1968

It is to the late 1960s and 1970s that we must turn to uncover the emergence of a major shift in the statutory/voluntary relationship. This does not imply that there was a drastic policy change which effectively wiped out what had gone before. (See Foucault, 1972, on the emergence of new discourses.)

The Social Work (Scotland) Act of 1968 and the developments which grew out of this were entirely predictable given the acceptance in post war legislation of the principle of universal, statutory services. Then in the 1960s, two governmental committees (McBoyle and Kilbrandon), one Children and Young Person's Act (1963) and one White Paper (Social Work and the Community, 1966) worked out the details of the new forms of service provision, and the basis for the new relationship between statutory and voluntary agencies. (English, 1988.)

The central proposition contained in the Social Work (Scotland) Act was that each local authority would be responsible to "promote social welfare, by making available advice, guidance and assistance on such a scale as may be appropriate for their area." (Section 12 (1) pp. 7-8.) Various circulars clarified this to explain that every person had a right to a service appropriate to his or her needs. Social work was to become a universal service - "one door for everyone to knock on"; for all people, not just the residuum. The role of the voluntary sector was defined an addition to the broad sweep of statutory services - to "supplement local authority work" and to be a

144

"stimulus to further progress". Under Section 10 of the Act, local authorities were given wide powers to contribute financially to voluntary organisations in the social welfare field. (The later Seebohm Report in England and Wales reflected similar arrangements.)

In the period leading up to the passing of the 1968 Act, many voluntary organisations expressed nervousness about their futures. Guild of Service Director, Janet Lusk, wrote in 1963 that she envisaged the possible redundancy of the agency's work in the future. If a statutory family service was set up, she predicted:-

> ... it is likely that such a family service will eventually cover all the work that the Guild of Service is doing just now for unmarried mothers, and their children, including adoption.[18]

Not surprisingly, after 1968 many voluntary organisations were forced to review their work and their future directions. Edinburgh Council of Social Service's review at this time led to a dramatic change in its functioning. It moved away from providing a casework service to adopting a community development model, servicing other agencies rather than providing services itself.[19] The Guild of Service's review began in 1973 and lasted for eighteen months. The outcome was less radical. The agency decided to change its constitution, bringing a greater staff voice onto decision making, and to shift service priorities in favour of specialisation - from adoption of babies towards home finding (finding homes for "hard to place" children) and from long term residential care towards moving children on to new placements.

Expansion of social work, 1970s -1980s

The 1968 Act proved a mixed blessing for voluntary child care agencies. The combined result of the 1968 Act and the 1975 reorganisation of local government was the creation of statutory services on a scale and of a quality hitherto unknown. Before and after Regionalisation, the new social work departments grew rapidly. Numbers of staff employed almost doubled between 1971 and 1981. (English, 1988, p. 124.) As one Director of a Scottish child care agency declared, "the boot is on the other foot now." Stone, 1985, p. 21.)

Perhaps surprisingly, the expansion of statutory services at this time did not mean the immediate disappearance of voluntary agencies en masse. Instead, many voluntary agencies like the Guild of Service did unprecedently well out of this period, as local authorities found themselves unprepared to meet the requirements of the new legislation, and as legislation brought with it an extension in social work in general. While local authority social work services expanded over the next twenty years, so did financial backing for voluntary sector social services.

This can be illustrated by examining the percentage figures for annual income to the Guild of Service/Family Care, comparing government sources of income with income from the agency's Thrift Shop. Here we can see that throughout the 1970s, both the agency's size, and its dependence on grant aid increased greatly. In the financial year 1977-78, grant aid was six times higher than Thrift Shop takings; by 1980-81, it was fourteen times higher. At the same time, funds received from private legacies and donations was rapidly decreasing. The financial year 1987-88 marks the peak for percentage of annual income received from government funding. Now almost seventy per cent of funds came from local or central government sources, and a tiny fraction (less than ten per cent) from the Thrift Shop. (See Figure 5.)

Statutory agencies in the late 1960s and 1970s, as I have stated, relied heavily on voluntary agencies to supplement their services. This was not because they wished to offer service users a choice, but because they needed a "stop gap" while they built up their own social work services. In the late 1960s, the Guild of Service assisted the new Midlothian Social Work Department with the adoptive placement of a backlog of babies and toddlers found to be living in residential care. At the same time, the Guild of Service handled all the adoptions for Clackmannan Social Work Department, which did not then have the expertise to provide its own adoptive service, and loaned staff to other agencies (including Aberdeen Children's Department) for short periods for staff training. Statutory agencies made widespread use of voluntary children's homes. By 1970, all the children living in Edzell Lodge were paid for by one or other local authority (which met two-thirds of the total cost of maintenance.) A study of residential care carried out in 1973 found that all the voluntary children's homes in Scotland were overcrowded. (Newman and Mackintosh, 1976.)

In the longer term, while making use of voluntary services, the new Social Work Departments were strengthening their own resources and expertise, in casework services, adoption and residential child care. Interviews with respondents who came from local authority settings to work at the Guild of Service in the 1970s confirm that although the agency still held onto its reputation as a centre of excellence, they found that the actual social work practice of the agency was by now of a similar standard to that of social work departments.[20] Meanwhile, voluntary agencies fought hard in the 1970s and 1980s to try to achieve a reasonable degree of consultation with statutory agencies with regard to planning of child care policy and practice.[21] (See Brenton, 1985, p. 128; Mordaunt, 1992.)

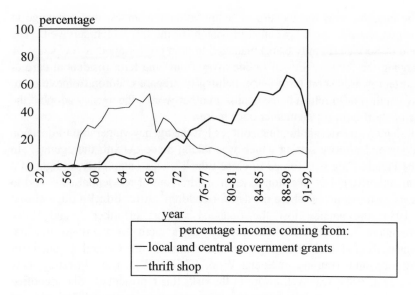

Source: Guild of Service/Family Care annual reports
Figure 5 Annual income: thrift shop and government grants,
Guild of Service/Family Care, 1952-1992

Mike Stone (1984) in a study of changes in child care in the period 1978 to 1984 identifies 1980 as the critical point for voluntary child care agencies. Up until then, in spite of increasing statutory provision, voluntary children's homes continued to have waiting lists, and to take an ever increasing percentage of children who were officially in the care of the local authority and paid for by statutory agencies. Then within a few years, voluntary children's homes throughout Scotland were faced with closure, as the tide turned away from residential care for children (most influential here was a study by Rowe and Lambert, 1973), and as the Social Work Departments found it cheaper and preferable to use their own accommodation. (Guild of Service and Barnardo's by 1981 were charging local authorities the full cost of maintenance of children in care). Stone expresses the change vividly:-

When change came it came suddenly with hurricane ferocity driving the voluntary fleet before it and overwhelming many caught by surprise ... Managers of those voluntary societies which had survived went off to the SWDs and saw officials and councillors for guidance, for some relief of hardship and to look for a role. But there was no master plan for the future and not much in the relief fund. (Stone, pp. 21-23.)

The outcome was the closure of many voluntary homes, and a change in direction towards more specialist provision for the few which survived. The Guild of Service (Family Care) managed to hold out for another few years by changing the focus of Edzell Lodge away from long term residential care of children towards short term work, helping to prepare children to move on to new families or to return home again. In other words, the agency adopted the role of short term supplementer once more.

Reliance on external funding sources left the agency vulnerable to decision making and priority setting which was taking place outwith the agency. In 1984 Family Care was forced to close Edzell Lodge completely, in light of a local authority policy decision to keep children out of residential care, and to use its own resources where needed for children. After Edzell Lodge closed in 1984, the agency lost the financial support of other Social Work Departments and found itself increasingly at the mercy of two major funders, Lothian Region and central government through the Central Council for Education and Training in Social Work (CCETSW). Kate Priestley, new Director in 1984, was well aware of the risks this represented. She identified that only the reasonably large voluntary organisations would be able to survive in the future - they would be able to "spread the risks and ride the rough times."[22] She tried therefore to negotiate a merger between Family Care and Aberlour Childcare Trust, as a way of broadening the base and strengthening the bargaining position of both agencies. However, after she resigned, merger plans were abandoned as being "unworkable".[23]

CCETSW's decision at the end of the 1980's to relocate the practice teaching unit in another agency coincided with Lothian Region (faced with rate capping by central government) cutting its grant to Family Care. The impact of this double blow to the agency was massive. The agency lost its funding, its ability to provide services, its student training and its status in the social work world all at the same time. The gap between income and expenditure began to grow at an alarming rate. By making staff redundant, and by eating into its financial reserves, the agency has been able to continue, although at a much reduced level. Staff have also worked hard to increase other means of funding, at times employing fund raisers to try to assist this process. The Thrift Shop income has risen again, and there have been efforts to try to get Regional Councils and Scottish Office to fund the adoption counselling services and Birth Link, the adoption contact register. The agency has also tried without a great measure of success to interest local industry in its work, and has been forced to consider charges for some of its services.[24]

Here we can see the inherent dangers in fulfilling a role of "gap-filling" in services for local authorities, and in becoming too dependent on government sources of income. Time limited supplementation may allow the agency to continue, but it does not provide conditions for long term development. Kramer (1981) argues:-

> Over a long period, supplementing or compensating for a lack of statutory resources is a weak rationale for a voluntary agency, which loses its distinctiveness by being just another non governmental public-service provider. (p. 251)

Kramer goes on to suggest that long term supplementation, by compensating for deficiencies in the statutory services, may displace other traditional voluntary roles, such as pioneer and advocate, and may deter or delay the implementation of governmental responsibility. This is the inevitable "catch-22" situation which Family Care has found itself in. Maintaining existing services meant that there were few spare resources either of money or of people to establish new services. Developments have therefore been limited to the small scale, incremental kind which I have already described.

Voluntary agencies in the 1990s

Social work departments throughout Scotland are currently reorganising to meet the requirements of yet more legislation, this time the NHS and Community Care Act of 1990. New buzz words such as "consumer choice" and "decentralisation of budgets" have entered the social work rhetoric, and local authorities are becoming "purchasers" and "monitors" instead of providers of care. Voluntary agencies, in turn, are being invited to compete with one another and the private and statutory sectors to see who can provide the most "cost-effective" services.

Stephen Maxwell (1989) from the Scottish Council of Voluntary Organisations sums up the difficult choices facing the voluntary sector:-

> ... It can refuse to commit itself to the market as defined by the government, in which case it must expect its public funding to decline. Or it can commit itself to the market, in which case it is colluding with, indeed actively facilitating, the replacement of public service provision by contracted out private or "third sector" provision on terms unfavourable to its clients. There is a third course which experience suggests is the one adopted by the majority of voluntary organisations - to engage with the market while protesting the need for a high level of public provision, on the principle that if you can't ride two horses at the

149

same time you've no damn business in the circus. (Maxwell, 1989, p. 5.)

Family Care's present Director, Jennifer Speirs, exemplifies this position. She believes that a strong statutory social work department is necessary, and sees the rightful role of the voluntary sector as a complement, not substitute for local authority services. Nevertheless she has had to embrace the new world, and has endeavoured to sell the Adoption Counselling service to statutory agencies, while at the same time reluctantly accepting the idea of seeking donations from clients for adoption searches.[25]

Substituting for statutory services has only be seen on a limited scale in Scotland to date, but it seems likely to continue and to increase in the future. Newham Social Services Department in England already contracts out its children and families' services to voluntary agencies, leaving its staff to concentrate on child protection duties. While this arrangement may seem advantageous to management (and to government), the implications for both statutory and voluntary agencies are huge. Voluntary agencies may find themselves caught up in restricted, short term contract work. Statutory social work will become more associated with a policing role, with all the preventive work and counselling (and perhaps even assessment eventually) being carried out elsewhere.

The overall outlook for welfare provision remains unclear. Some of the ideas may bring about an improvement in the delivery of services. The greater emphasis on consumer involvement and choice, and the stress on participation and devolvement of power seems likely to lead to more "user friendly" services in the future. But in reality, these changes are being introduced in an environment of cuts in funding and the removal of control from local to central government. Clark (1991) warns voluntary agencies to be careful "that what is offered as *partnership* does not turn out to be domestication enforced by the choke-collar of the service contract." (p. 172.)

Summary

This chapter has described in some detail the battle which has taken place between voluntary and statutory welfare discourses, and the gradual transformation from a nineteenth century model of welfare provision based on voluntarist principles to a twentieth century model which assumes a high level of statutory control and regulation of service provision. This battle has been principally about "who is allowed to speak?" (Foucault, 1972), that is, who is in charge of the welfare discourse? I have argued that in spite of a recent policy shift towards non-statutory service delivery, management and control of the welfare discourse remain primarily in governmental hands.

Family Care stands as an example of an agency which has achieved a degree of excellence in its service delivery. It has pioneered new approaches and encouraged others, including statutory agencies, to make improvements and to take on new ideas. But it also illustrates the vulnerabilities in a voluntary agency - its inability to make decisive changes as it became caught up in its own professionalised, institutionalised system; its ineffectiveness at raising funds for projects which are unpopular or "out of fashion" with current trends in social work; its potential for marginality given its small scale provision of services; its non-participative, hierarchical organisation, and lack of user involvement in decision making processes.

I hope that a mixed economy of welfare will survive, and I agree with Matthews' (1992) assertion that the voluntary sector *depends* on good statutory welfare provision:-

> ... for a balanced provision to emerge, it must be based not on false notions of welfare pluralism or the mirage of free choice between equally known and valuable services, but rather on a mixed economy based on a reappraisal of the relative strengths and weaknesses of the statutory as against the voluntary sector, and on a genuine attempt to harness the strength of advocacy and specialism which are the hallmarks of voluntary bodies and the quest for equity which lies at the heart of state provision. (Matthews, 1989, p. 156.)

Notes

1. Hansard, Parliamentary Debates (House of Lords) 5th ser., vol. 163, col. 119 (23 June 1949).
2. The Poor Law Commission (1905-1909) produced two reports, a Majority Report which reflected the views of the Charity Organisation Society and was written largely by Helen Bosanquet, and a Minority Report, produced by Beatrice and Sidney Webb. See McBriar (1987).
3. N. Fowler (1984), Speech to Local Authority Social Services Conference, quoted in Webb and Wistow (1987).
4. Scottish Council for Voluntary Organisations, in *The Herald*, 23-08-94.
5. Interview, 04-04-90.
6. Interview with Kate Priestley, 20-02-91.
7. Lothian Regional Council Social Work Department (1981) policy document, "A Time of Change".
8. Interview, 18-02-91.

Continued

9. Interview, 19-03-91.
10. Interview, 18-03-91.
11. Interview, 21-03-91, and Annual Report, 1991-1992.
12. Interview with Janet Lusk, 25-05-90.
13. Interview, 18-02-91.
14. Interview, 18-02-91.
15. For example, 1870 Education Act; 1872 Public Health Act; 1875 Criminal Law Amendment Act.
16. Interview, 12-11-89.
17. Interview, 26-03-90.
18. Annual Report, 1965.
19. Interview, 03-06-92.
20. Two interviews, 21-02-91, and one interview, 06-03-91.
21. Interview with Janet Lusk, 28-05-92.
22. Interview with Kate Priestley, 10-06-91.
23. Interview, 24-06-91.
24. Interviews, 18-03-91 and 19-03-91.
25. Interview with Jennifer Speirs, 02-07-91.

8 Conclusion

Overview

This chapter takes me back to my initial question - what is the task of social work? I have argued that in the early days of this agency, there was a great variety of work encompassed by the term "social work". Housing associations, casework agencies, rescue societies, children's charities, and even the public workhouse/poorhouse could all be described as social work institutions. What underpinned this social work activity was an assumption that the state should have a minimal role in intervening in the lives of individuals. Beyond this statement, social work was in effect "up for grabs", its task and its direction by no means self-evident.

At the end of the nineteenth century and beginning of the twentieth century, a general transformation took place, as a new relationship between the individual and the state was worked out. Now there was an acceptance of a legitimate role for the state in regulating and monitoring individuals' behaviour, and a host of new professionals emerged to take on responsibility for this statutory intervention. The struggle to create the professional social work task must be understood as part of this development towards greater "policing" of individuals and families in a "disciplinary society." (Foucault, 1977; Donzelot, 1980.)

With the professionalisation of social work, the social work task was reconstituted to become a narrowly-focused activity carried out by professionally trained workers under the control and legitimation of the state. In this agency, that meant certain types of activity had to go (principally vigilance work), and only qualified workers were allowed to work with service users. Quite literally, the task of social work shifted *from public streets to private lives*, as personal interviews and counselling overtook patrolling and public work on the streets.

The professional social work task was made possible by the creation of a new discourse on social work, one which drew heavily on a body of knowledge and skills drawn from psychology and psycho-analysis, and which modelled itself on "scientific" principles. At the same time, older, Christian values and ethics were re-packaged and translated into professional social work language.

As "disciplinary power" in society has continued to grow, so social work has been incorporated steadily into statutory mechanisms. Not only has the state won the right to intervene in the lives of individuals, it has effectively taken control over how this should be carried out and by whom. Voluntary social work agencies cannot now function without some measure of control over their activities by the local authority and by the legislature. Even in the era of "care in the community", it is the local authority which inspects voluntary institutions and give out contracts for work on its behalf. Social work education bears witness to this transformation. Teaching student social workers is no longer the prerogative of research-led academic institutions. Now employers (crucially, local authorities) have a large say in how courses are run, and central government has chosen through the Central Council (CCETSW) to have greater involvement in setting priorities and agendas for social work training.

Alongside these changes, the task of social work has become increasingly legalistic, bureaucratic and technical. Social work practice has become more regulatory, more inspectorial, and more "masculine" in style, while the more "feminine", counselling aspects of social work are in the process of being separated off into private or voluntary counselling agencies. One major consequence of the drive for technical skill and specialist knowledge is that the idea of generic social work has been discredited. It is no longer reasonable to talk about "transferable skills" in a world in which the sheer volume of specialist knowledge centred on procedures and legislation continues to grow.

But what of the continuities in social work? And what of the struggles, contradictions and disagreements which have taken place along the way, all of which have mitigated against any wholescale transformation, and which continue to limit the impact of change? Are all the changes which I have described necessarily positive or negative? Might there not be quite mixed and surprising consequences for those of us involved in social work? Since I have argued throughout this book that discourses have the capacity to be contradictory, oppositional, and relative, it is the complexity of the social work discourse which I wish to foreground in my final analysis.

Continuities within the social work discourse

I have argued that in its early days, the task of social work was defined in terms of a minimal role for the state in providing basic support and shelter for those unable to care for themselves. The principle of "less-eligibility" meant that any help offered was at as low a level as possible, to prevent individuals from becoming dependent and relinquishing their own responsibilities. I have also proposed that a shift took place with the state gradually assuming responsibility for a wide number of needs and functions previously met by the family or the voluntary sector.

However, one of the facts which this case study has highlighted is that in spite of the rhetoric about the welfare state and about the universality of services, this was *never* a reality. Service provision in social work was never at a level where this goal could be attainable, and the principle of means-testing of welfare benefits was never dismantled. (See Chapter 7.) In other words, the continuities have been as fundamental as the changes which have taken place.

Recent community care legislation which introduces financial assessments of clients' ability to pay for services has shattered any remaining myths about social services being available for all as of right. Social work in the future seems set to split between its inspectorial function, targeted at all of society, and its social care function, focused on "the residue" who are unable to pay for care through insurance schemes and private means.

There are other continuities within the social work discourse which are just as fundamental to the social work task. I have argued in Chapter 2 that women and children continue to be designated as being in need of special surveillance, and special care/control. This may have positive implications for women and children, who are disadvantaged in terms of power in society and who may therefore need a level of protection against male violence and institutional sexism. However, this approach also has huge implications for women in particular in terms of allowing the sexual double standard to go unchallenged, and treating women in an unfair, discriminatory manner. Social work is again beginning to tackle the issue of changing men - a goal which was central to the vigilance movement supporters - as a new feminist critique of masculinity is struggling to be heard within social work.

There are a number of other persistent themes which are fundamental to social work's value-base. As I have described in Chapter 3, these include ideas about the individual, the community and service to others. I have no doubt that these themes have been re-interpreted over time, but I agree with Foucault (1976) that there are strong continuities not only in the way in which subjects are created in discourse (that is, principally in the role of victims), but also in the practices themselves which have been instituted to deal with service users (that is, assessment and observation). Social work's stress on client self-determination (re-defined today as "empowerment" of clients), and its emphasis on working with individuals and families, has strong connections with nineteenth century ideas about individual self-help and about "helpable" cases. Although for a time in the 1970s social work expanded its horizons to include group work and community work approaches, it never seriously moved away from its concentration on individual and family solutions to what have often been structural problems, rooted in poverty and inequality rather than individual deficiency or mismanagement.

There are, of course, examples of agencies which do not fit this privatised, individualised picture. There are a growing number of voluntary agencies and self-help groups striving to challenge existing systems of welfare provision. There are also some statutory projects which seek to support and empower various underprivileged groups, including feminist social work initiatives and innovative work with black service users and those with learning difficulties. (See Langan and Day, 1992.) But most of these more radical projects are not under the auspices of statutory social work as such. They may be community work projects (which have consistently adopted a more radical approach) or small scale social work initiatives which have little impact on core service provision.

The contradictory task of social work

The shift towards a "disciplinary society" may be interpreted in different ways. It can be regarded as positive and to be welcomed. Women and children are no longer viewed as solely the property of husbands and fathers, and intervention has brought with it the possibility of protection and support for less powerful family members. On the other hand, the enlarging of the educative/preventive role has given the new psy professionals a much greater potential for involvement and control in the lives of all citizens, not simply those labelled as troublesome or in difficulty. This reflects the reality that discourses operate in contradictory ways.

I have argued in Chapter 6 that women's relationship with the social work discourse is fraught with contradiction. Women have tended to be both service users and service deliverers, paid and unpaid, qualified and unqualified. The only area of social work in which women do not predominate is senior management, and here too in the voluntary sector in Scotland women have been well represented. If social work is a sexist and oppressive institution, then it has largely been an oppression carried out by women on women. This raises important dilemmas for us women in social work.

"The state" itself operates in contradictory ways. The Children Act of 1989 illustrates a compromise between the need to protect children from danger while at the same time protecting the privacy of the family from unwarranted interventions. (Parton, 1991, p. 3.) The complexities do not end here. There are substantial differences between "the state" as it is encountered at central government and local government level, and real differences between different local authorities' policies. This means that one Social Work Department in Scotland (Highland Region) continued to use residential care for children while another (Fife) found itself in 1993 the subject of a governmental enquiry into its policy of keeping children out of residential institutions.

Sometimes the consequences of the development of different discourses in social work have been positive for some, and negative for others. As I have described in Chapters 4 and 5, the professionalisation process brought higher status and higher salaries for paid staff, but effectively squeezed out for a time the contribution of unpaid workers. Although volunteers are now back on the social work scene, social work professionals still guard carefully their special expertise and their right to control and limit the work of volunteers. This relationality is another example of the contradiction within discourse.

The future for social work?

When I began interviewing respondents in 1989 for my case study of Family Care, social work was on the verge of a new set of changes which would consolidate a shift already in motion - a shift which I have described as being towards a more inspectorial, technical social work task. These changes were embodied in the Children Act of 1989, and in the NHS and Community Care Act of 1990 (implemented in April 1993), and are reflected in anticipated legislation for children in Scotland. As part of these legislative changes, organisation and delivery of social work services in Scotland has been altered radically. Departments have been reorganised into specialist teams based on a district model, and there has been a split between purchaser and provider roles in social work. Clients are now "consumers", and social workers are brokers in a market of care, striving to maintain their status faced with new challenges from other "care managers" - occupational therapists, district nurses and community psychiatric nurses. Social workers, whether in child care, mental health or community care settings, are finding their jobs increasingly circumscribed and designated in procedural terms.

The picture I have presented here may seem overly bleak - that was not my intention. On the contrary I believe that there are hopeful signs for social work, and I wish to consider these now.

Mainstream social work has taken on board some important issues in recent years, and is currently working to put these into practice. I include here attempts to carry out not just ethnically sensitive practice, but anti-discriminatory and anti-oppressive practice. Feminist and anti-racist ideas and research have played a key role in informing this practice. We may feel that equal opportunities policies as they are currently instituted do not go far enough, and that there is sometimes more "political correctness" than commitment to real change. But I prefer to be optimistic that at least these matters are on the agenda for social work, and that negotiation and challenge is therefore possible.

Likewise, the beginnings of attempts to involve service users in service provision must be applauded. It is right that there should be access to files held on clients, and that clients should be drawn into the decision making processes on individual cases and on agency policy. We may feel sceptical about the motives for introducing such changes. But that should not prevent us from using the opportunity to press for even more radical changes here.

I also welcome the explosion in voluntary advocacy and self-help groups in recent years. I believe that pressure groups like these have a vital role to play in challenging and amending social welfare policy and practice, as well as providing a useful service by empowering and supporting their members.

Final words

I believe in the end that it is social work's diversity and its complexity which gives me most cause for optimism. If social work is a polymorphous phenomenon as I have suggested; if negotiation, contestation and resistance are endemic in social work's formation; then change is possible. It is up to us to push for the kind of social work task with which we wish to be associated.

Appendix: Research methods

Documentary sources

I critically studied a wide variety of internal agency material and external sources to broaden my understanding of the context within which Family Care was operating. Documentary evidence served different purposes at different stages of the research process.

Primary sources included:-

1   Agency Annual Reports, committee minutes, short histories of Family Care written by a director and committee chairman, and case records.

2   Documentary material from other relevant agencies - the National Vigilance Association (NVA) and the Scottish Council for Single Parents (SCSP). NVA records are held in the Fawcett Library in London; SCSP archives are held at the agency's headquarters in Edinburgh.

Internal agency records helped me in the early stages of the research process to build up a background picture of the agency's history - its philosophy and work practices. This was particularly important for the period before 1929, from which there was no one still alive whom I could interview. When the interviews began, agency records were useful in allowing me to cross check what respondents were telling me. I was able to verify dates, chronology and factual information, vitally important when interviewing respondents about events which had taken place in the past.

Documents offered far more, however, than simple verification. They offered real evidence and first hand examples of events in process, untainted by post hoc rationalisation or explanation. This does not suggest that documents are somehow more "truthful" than verbal accounts. Documents are full of their own value judgements, and provide only a partial account of what has actually taken place. (Platt, 1981a.) This make them all the more interesting to the researcher - they become an ongoing research tool, and a source to be exploited throughout the research process. Foucault argues that a document is not a window through which deeper meanings can be interpreted. It is "a positive material entity in itself, conditioned by the same regulative mechanisms that determine social practices." (Foucault, 1972, p. 138.)

Agency records of two key external agencies, the NVA in London and the Scottish Council for Single Parents (formerly the Scottish Council for the Unmarried Mother and her Child, SCUM) were helpful in filling in gaps and in placing Family Care's history in a wider context. The NVA archives were able to tell me what had happened to the NVA nationally. The SCUM records added to my understanding of the field of moral welfare in the 1940s and 1950s, and acted as a point of verification for what the Guild of Service/Family Care was saying about itself.

Secondary sources included:-

1   Histories of other voluntary organisations - including Dr. Barnardo's, Royal Scottish Society for the Prevention of Cruelty to Children, Quarrier's Homes, Edinburgh Council of Social Service, Claremont Park Mother and Baby Home, Scottish Marriage Guidance, Church of Scotland, National Council for Single Parents. Scottish material is available at the Edinburgh Central Library.

2   Histories of social work itself - histories of child care, moral welfare work, social work education, the probation service, and voluntary and statutory social work.

3   Other relevant histories - of Magdalene homes, of prostitution, of police women, of sexuality, of family violence, of the medical care of pregnant women, of penal strategies, of the family, of women and mental health, of feminism.

Secondary sources were useful in placing Family Care's development in a wider context - in the world of voluntary organisations and in the world of social work. However, secondary sources did not always live up to my

160

expectations of them, and I had to read widely in order to feel adequately informed of my subject and its context.

I was disappointed in the quality of presentation and analysis of much of the histories of voluntary organisations which I read. These histories tended to be impressionistic and descriptive, relying on narrative accounts and uncritical swatches of biographical material about the key figures involved in the organisations. There were a number of exceptions. The work of Brenton (1985), Finlayson (1990) and Prochaska (1980 and 1988) were excellent in their breadth of coverage and in their attention to voluntary sector issues.

While histories of voluntary organisations were limited in their usefulness, general histories of social work were also less than satisfying. Many histories of social work adopt an evolutionary, linear approach, in which there is a notion of steady progress towards an ever-improving social work product. There is no indication of the conflict which accompanied these changes, and no analysis of competing interests of groups involved in the process. More than this, many histories are told from the perspective of statutory, English social work settings, with little attention to either the voluntary sector or the Scottish social work scene and legislation. Where the voluntary sector is mentioned, it is most typically in terms of a reference to the Charity Organisation Society, at which point voluntary agency activity seems to disappear from the public view for the next sixty years or so. The differing Scottish social work pattern is sometimes ignored completely; at other times, it merits a disclaiming paragraph. However, Cooper (1983), English (1988), Thane (1982), and Walton (1975) contributed to my general understanding of the development of social work in Scotland.

Some of the most informative histories which I read were those which were only tangentially related to my research topic, but which adopted a strong theoretical position. Histories which drew on Foucauldian concepts enabled me to clarify my own theoretical framework. Here I include the work of Garland (1985), Mahood (1990), Mort (1987), Oakley (1984), Rose (1985) and Weeks (1981).

I also found the blossoming literature of oral histories and accounts of women's lives useful in identifying some broad subject-areas which I might explore with respondents. These have included the impact of the Second World War; women's changing employment pattern; domestic service; women and caring; women's attitudes towards sexual behaviour; feminism.

Interviews

I carried out 80 interviews in total and communicated by letter with a further

6 respondents. Of this total number, 61 were internal respondents - Directors, committee members, social workers and administrators who have worked at Family Care. Two interviews were carried out with relatives of key agency figures, now dead; and I interviewed a foster parent who approached me early in the research. I also interviewed 16 external respondents who knew the agency well and who had themselves played a part in the development of social work in Scotland. (See Figure 6.)

Much of what has been written in conventional social science text books on interviewing bears little resemblance to my interview process. Firstly, my respondents were not a sample in any traditional sense. I interviewed *all* of those who were available from the early period, and got in touch with all those from the later period whose addresses I could get hold of, sometimes contacting individuals on the recommendation of other respondents (the "snowball" technique), and at other times carrying out some detective work of my own. This approach produced a very diverse grouping of respondents, who had from one to twenty two years experience with the agency I was studying.

Secondly, interviews were neither structured surveys using standard questions, nor open ended, unstructured conversations as in an oral history technique. Quite simply, they were semi-structured. I had some specific questions I wished to put to each respondent, but the main part of the interview was designed to be open enough to allow for the respondent to tell her/his own story - whatever was most significant for each of them about the time of their association with Family Care.

In order to facilitate this process, I prepared well in advance of the interview. I sent respondents a short but informative resume of my areas of interest prior to the interview, to give them time to reflect and prepare for the interview. This approach worked well. It served to reduce anxiety about the interview, and allowed respondents time to think about the past, to discuss it with family and friends, and even in some cases, to retrieve old documents and papers which they felt that I might be interested in. I also gave priority to preparation for each individual interview, anticipating subjects which we might discuss, and having a tool kit of prompts and suggestions (including dates, issues, material from other interviews) that I might draw on which would enable the respondent to get in touch with their memories and their feelings.

The interview took the shape of an informed discussion. I contributed to the discussion, and fed in, where appropriate, ideas and issues raised by other respondents. This was not, however, a normal conversation following the rules of conventional social intercourse. My role was clearly that of an informed listener and questioner. Because I did not wish to influence the

Internal interviews

  5   Directors (all the Directors from 1929 onwards)

27   Social Workers (a sample from 1946 onwards)

  4   Admin/Finance Officers (all from 1942 onwards)

  6   Executive Committee Chairmen* (all from 1945 onwards)

19   Committee Members (a sample from 1946 onwards)

  2   Relatives of key Executive Committee Members

  1   Foster Parent

External interviews

  3   Local Authority Social Workers (Children's Department and Lothian Regional Council Social Work Department)

  4   Edinburgh University Lecturers/tutors

  1   Former Scottish Council for Single Parents Director

  1   Scottish Adoption Association Director

  2   Former Simpson's Maternity Hospital Social Workers

  1   Brook Advisory Service Director

  1   Edinburgh Council of Social Service Director

  2   Scottish Episcopal Church Clergymen

  1   New College Lecturer/tutor

Correspondents

  2   Children's Officers

  1   Social Worker from Lothian Region Social Work Department

  1   Former Edinburgh University Tutor

  2   Former Family Care Social Workers

Refusals

  6   Social workers now living in England did not respond to my letter

  3   Living in or near Edinburgh chose not to respond

  1   Social worker declined to be interviewed

Total sample 86 respondents

(Note: the title "Chairman" was used by all those who had chaired the Executive Committee even though most were women.)

Figure 6 Respondents, internal and external, 1990-1992

respondent's contribution, I refused to answer the "what do *you* think?" questions, and instead turned this back onto respondents. Over and above the specific material related to the respondents' experience of Family Care, I also sought respondents' views on the wider research issues, and I invited them to comment on, and interpret their experience.

Most interviews were tape recorded, after seeking permission from the respondents. This made it easier for me to actively listen in the interviews, and once the respondents had relaxed and forgotten about the tape recorder, it also served to reduce the distance between me as researcher and the respondent as interviewee.

The interview process - the presentation, structure and style which I chose to adopt - reflects both my own past experience and my theoretical orientation, informed by three separate but inter-related strands: the oral/life history method, feminist research, and social work principles and practice.

The oral history/life history method stresses the importance of enabling respondents to actively engage in the research process and to tell their own stories. (Thomson, 1981.) Feminist research develops this approach and adds a feminist dimension to it. Oakley (1981) argues against objectivity and detachment in interviewing, because what is good for interviewers may not be good for interviewees. She proposes a feminist mode of interviewing that requires personal responsiveness and involvement on the part of the interviewer. She suggests that personal involvement is more than dangerous bias - "it is the condition under which people come to know each other and admit others into their lives." (p. 58)

From this perspective, what may have been regarded as a source of potential danger in my research - the fact that I was an "insider" carrying out the research - became a positive asset. As a social worker, as a women and as a mother, I was able to make personal connections with what respondents were telling me. I was able to get *behind* what respondents are saying - to pick up cues and ask supplementary questions, and really listen to what was being said. At the same time, by being open to the feelings and subjectivities of others, I found myself confronting my own feelings and subjectivity. Stanley and Wise (1983) have indicated that the research process can be a consciousness raising experience, raising the levels of awareness of both the researcher and the researched.

The third underlying thread which inevitably had an impact on the research method and process has been my experience of counselling and interviewing clients. Social work principles impress on us the value of creating a warm and safe environment in counselling; of listening empathetically to what is said; of being prepared to "start where the client is"; of seeking clarification and giving feedback. My model therefore owes much to Rogerian ideas

164

about person centred counselling. (Rogers, 1951.) This is not to suggest that I counselled respondents - clearly, I did not. But the general approach has been useful in   conducting interviews which aim to get in touch with respondents' feelings as well as factual information.

Two final research strategies which I found useful deserve a mention - Dexter (1970) and his notion of "elite" or "specialised" interviewing, and Platt's (1981b) study of interviewing one's peers.

Confidentiality

While wanting to be as open as possible about the research product, I have endeavoured to preserve confidentiality in the research and in this book. This has been achieved in a number of ways.

First, I chose not to interview current members of staff and committee members, except for the current Director and Secretary/Treasurer. This was in recognition of the fact that I was writing a history, and that present day material was too recent, and perhaps too controversial.

Second, I deliberately sought to verify statements made to me, either through documentary investigation, or by discussing material with another respondent, without, of course, naming or implicating the source of my information. On occasions I chose not to use a sensitive piece of information; at other times, it seemed too vital to be missed out.

Third, in writing up the research, I have chosen to name only the Directors/Organising Secretaries; all other respondents are identified by the date of our meeting.   The Directors are named in part because it is a matter of public record that they held these posts. But more importantly, I have named them because their contribution has been so significant, and I wish to give value to their work.

Service user perspectives

I interviewed only one service user, and this was after she made contact with me. The decision not to interview service users (clients) was a decision made only after a great deal of thought. During the course of interviewing staff and committee members, and as the focus of the research project developed, I came to understand that I was not in the business of assessing whether one kind of social work activity was more or less effective than another. Neither was I primarily concerned with changes in social attitudes, and hence with a wide cross section of perceptions of these changes.

But there is an added dimension here. One of the characterising features of social work is that it has *not* been set up as a self help/ mutual aid institution in which intervention is geared towards client demand. Routinely, need has been identified and solutions proposed by people other than clients - principally middle class "experts" and "knowledgeable" lay people. In the context of Family Care, in common with most professional social work agencies, the task of social work is in the hands of the service providers, not the service users, and this has remained a constant feature throughout its eighty year history. This means that it is to the service providers and managers I had to turn to find the *subjects* (Foucault, 1972) in the social work discourse, and in my research project.

Accepting that the task of social work has been and is under the control of the service providers, there are ways of uncovering the implications of this without recourse to client interviews. From interviews with social workers, managers and those who have worked closely with the agency, as well as from case records, it is possible to learn about the clients themselves (who are the clients? where do they come from? what problems do they bring?); about the relationship between social workers and clients (what do they call each other? what information do they share with each other? how does the social worker record their interaction?); and about the nature and outcome of the intervention (are there times when one outcome seems to be favoured over another? does this change over time? how far is this unique to Family Care or part of a wider pattern?)

There is much good, current research available on clients' experiences of social work intervention. (See Rees and Wallace, 1982; Cheetham et al, 1992.) There are also a number of contemporary accounts and research studies carried out by social workers at, or in connection with their work at the Guild of Service/Family Care. (See McWhinnie, 1967, on experiences of adoption; Hopkinson, 1976, and Lamotte, 1981, on single mothers; Humphries, 1976, and McCaw and Sage, 1986, on volunteers and single parent families; McCaw and McGuire, 1980, on volunteers of children in care; Bouchier, Lambert and Triseliotis, 1991, on birth mothers.)

Participant observation

Although this research project was not an exercise in participant observation in the strict sense, I have nevertheless had an unusually high degree of involvement in the agency throughout the research process. I worked for the agency for seven years before starting the research, and indeed spent the first year of the research while still an employee of the agency. After then, I continued to have regular contact with the agency, by going in to look at agency records, by informal conversation with staff members, and by attending annual general meetings.

This continued involvement with the agency allowed me to keep up to date with agency concerns and issues. It also enabled me to check out informally some of the ideas coming up in the research, and to feed back provisional findings to agency staff. My research therefore, in a limited way, took on the character of an action research project, since I was able to contribute to debates taking place in the agency about its future directions.

Quantitative data

Although the main thrust in this research has been towards qualitative research, statistics and graphs have been used to evidence specific statements being made and to place the Family Care material in its wider context. This has made it possible to detect broader trends (for example, in illegitimacy figures, or in women's paid employment) and has brought an objectivity to the study which would not otherwise have been possible.

Summary

My research method was, in conclusion, to pull together a synthesis of documentary and interview research material, from internal and external sources, building on what I already knew as a social work practitioner and teacher, and basing my analysis on an open interaction between my own perspectives and those of my respondents. This has not, therefore, been a study in which concepts have simply "emerged" out of the data, in the manner of grounded theory. (Glaser and Strauss, 1967.) Neither has it been a project in which I have assumed full control of the subject and its analysis, as is typical of most conventional positivist research. Instead, I have drawn on insights from feminist and life/oral history research traditions, aiming at an approach which is both "theoretically alive, and substantially grounded in social reality. (Thompson, 1981, p. 294.)

Bibliography

Abrams, P. (1982), *Historical Sociology*, Open Books Publishing, London.

Acton, W. (1870), "Prostitution considered in its Social and Sanitary Aspects", in Jeffreys, S. (1987), *The Sexuality Debates*, Routledge and Kegan Paul, London, pp. 24-56.

Adler, A. (1924), *The Practice and Theory of Individual Psychology*, Kegan Paul, Trench, Trubner, New York.

Alexander, L.B. (1972), "Social Work's Freudian Deluge : Myth or Reality?", *Social Service Review*, 46, pp. 517-38.

Alexander, P. (1988), "Prostitution : A Difficult Issue for Feminists", in Delacoste F. and Alexander, P. (eds), *Sex Work. Writings by Women in the Sex Industry*, Virago, London.

Ashford, S. and Timms, N. (1990), "Values in Social Work : investigations of the practice of family placement", *British Journal of Social Work*, 20, pp. 1-20.

Aves Report (1969), *The Voluntary Worker in the Social Services*, National Institute for Social Work Training, London.

Bailey, R. and Brake, M. (1975), *Radical Social Work*, Edward Arnold, London.

Balbernie, R. (1966), *Residential Work with Children*, Pergamon Press, London.

Bamford, T. (1990), *The Future of Social Work*, MacMillan, London.

Banks, O. (1981), *Faces of Feminism*, Martin Robertson, Oxford.

Banks, O. (1985), *Biographical Dictionary of British Feminists, 1800- 1930*, Wheatsheaf Books, Sussex.

Banks, O. (1986), *Becoming a Feminist*, Wheatsheaf Books, Sussex.

Barclay Committee (1982), *Social Workers : their Roles and Tasks*, Bedford Square Press, London.

Barrett, M. and McIntosh, M. (1982), *The Anti-social Family*, Verso, London.

Becker, H.S. (1962), "The Nature of a Profession", in Henry, H.B. (ed), *Education for the Professions*, National Society for the Study of Education, Illinois.

Behlmer, G.K. (1982), *Child Abuse and Moral Reform in England, 1870-1908*, Stanford University Press, Stanford.

Bennett, F. et al. (1981), "Feminists - the Degenerates of the Social?", *Politics and Power*, 3.

Beresford, P. and Croft, S., "Welfare Pluralism : the new face of Fabianism", *Critical Social Policy*, 9, Spring.

Berger, P.L. and Luckman, T. (1967), *The Social Construction of Reality*, Penguin, London.

Berger, P.L. (1969), *The Social Reality of Religion*, Faber and Faber, London.

Berger, P.L. and Neuhaus, R.J. (1977), *To Empower People : The Role of Mediating Structures in Public Policy*, American Enterprise, Washington, D.C.

Bernauer, J. and Rasmussen, D. (1988), *The Final Foucault*, MIT Press, Cambridge.

Bertaux, D. (1981), *Biography and Society*, Sage, Beverly Hills.

Bland, L. and Mort, F. (1984), "Look out for the Good Time Girl - Dangerous Sexualities as a Threat to National Health", in *Formations of Nation and People*, London.

Bland, L. (1987), "The Married Woman, the New Woman and the Feminist. Sexual Politics in the 1890s", in Rendall, J., (ed), *Equal or Different. Women's Politics, 1800-1914*, Basil Blackwell, Oxford.

Borrowdale, A. (1989), *A Woman's Work. Changing Christian Attitudes*, SPCK, London.

Bouchier, P., Lambert, L. and Triseliotis, J. (1991), *Parting with a Child for Adoption. The Mother's Perspective*, BAAF, London.

Bowlby, J. (1941), *Maternal Care and Mental Health*, World Health Organisation.

Bowlby, J. (1953), *Childcare and the Growth of Love*, Pelican Books, Middlesex.

Bowlby, J. (1979), *The Making and Breaking of Affectional Bonds*, Tavistock, London.

Boyd, K.M. (1980), *Scottish Church Attitudes to Sex, Marriage and the Family, 1850-1914*, John Donald, Edinburgh.

Brenton, M. (1985), *The Voluntary Sector in British Social Services*, Longman, London.

169

Bristow, E.J. (1977), *Vice and Vigilance*, Gill and Macmillan, London.

Brittain, V. (1953), *Lady into Woman*, Andrew Dakers, London.

Brook, E. and Davis, A. (1985), *Women, the Family and Social Work*, Tavistock, London.

Brown, C. (1987), *The Social History of Religion in Scotland since 1730*, Methuen, London.

Bruce, N., Mitchell, A. and Priestley, K. (1988), *Truth and the Child*, Family Care, Edinburgh.

Burlingham, D. and Freud, A. (1944), *Infants without Families*, Allen and Unwin, London.

Butler, J. (1881), *Social Purity*, Dyer Brothers, London.

Campbell, A. (1981), *Girl Delinquents*, Basil Blackwell, Oxford.

Caring for People. Community Care in the Next Decade and Beyond (1989), HMSO Cm 849, London.

Carlen, P. (1983), *Women's Imprisonment*, Routledge, London.

Carlen, P. (1985), *Criminal Women*, Polity Press and Basil Blackwell, Cambridge.

Carr-Saunders, A.M. (1965), "Metropolitan Conditions and Traditional Professional Relationships", in Fisher, R.M. (ed), *The Metropolitis in Modern Life*, Doubleday and Co., pp. 279-287.

Casburn, M. (1979), *Girls will be Girls - Sexism and Juvenile Justice in a London Borough*, Women's Resource and Research Centre, London.

CCETSW (1989), *Requirements and Regulations for the Diploma in Social Work*, Paper 30, CCETSW, London.

Chafetz, J.S. (1972), "Women in Social Work", *Social Work*, 17 (5) Sept.

Chambers, C.A. (1986), "Women in the Creation of the Profession of Social Work", *Social Service Review*, March, pp. 1-33.

Chambers, R. (1959), "Professionalism in Social Work", in Wootten, B., *Social Science and Social Pathology*, Allen and Unwin, London.

Chaplin, J. (1988), *Feminist Counselling in Action*, Sage, London.

Cheetham, J., Fuller, R., McIvor, G., Petch, A. (1992), *Evaluating Social Work Effectiveness*, OU Press, Buckingham.

Clark, C.L. (1991), *Theory and Practice in Voluntary Social Action*, Avebury, Aldershot.

Clyde Committee (1946), *Committee on Homeless Children*, Cmd 6911, HMSO, Edinburgh.

Cobbold, H.M. (1935), *The District Visitor*, SPCK, London.

Cooper, D. (1994), "Productive, Relational and Everywhere? Conceptualising Power and Resistance within Foucauldian Feminism", in *Sociology*, 28, 2, pp. 435-454.

Conrad, P. and Schneider, J.W. (1980), *Deviance and Medicalisation : From Badness to Sickness*, C.V. Mosby, London.

Coote, W. (1910), *A Vision of Fulfilment*, NVA, London.

Coote, W. (1916), *A Romance of Philanthropy*, NVA, London.

Crabbie, V. and Keay, O. (1985), *The Story of Claremont Park. The Edinburgh Home for Mothers and Infants*, Edinburgh.

Curtis Committee, *Care of Children Committee*, Cmd 6922, HMSO, London.

Dale, J. and Foster, P. (1986), *Feminists and State Welfare*, Routledge and Kegan Paul, London.

Davis, A. and Brook, E. (1985), "Women and Social Work", in Brook, E. and Davis, A. (eds), *Women, the Family and Social Work*, Tavistock, London.

Delmar, R. (1986), "What is Feminism?" in Mitchell, J. and Oakley, A. (eds), *What is Feminism?*, Basil Blackwell, Oxford.

Dexter, L.A. (1970), *Elite and Specialised Interviewing*, Northwestern University Press, Evanston.

Dingwall, R., Eekelaar, J. and Murray, T. (1983), *The Protection of Children: State Intervention and Family Life*, Basil Blackwell, Oxford.

Dockar-Drysdale, B. (1968), *Therapy in Child Care*, Longman, London.

Dominelli, L. (1988), *Anti-Racist Social Work,* MacMillan, London.

Dominelli, L. and McLeod, E. (1989), *Feminist Social Work*, MacMillan, London.

Donzelot, J. (1980), *The Policing of Families*, Hutchinson, London.

Drucker, D. (1989), *The New Realities*, Heinemann, London.

Drummond, A.L. and Bulloch, J. (1973), *The Scottish Church 1688-1843*, Saint Andrew Press, Edinburgh.

Du Bois, B. (1983) "Passionate Scholarship : notes on values, knowing and method in feminist social science", in Bowles, G. and Duelli Klein, R. (eds) *Theories of Women's Studies*, Routledge and Kegan Paul, London.

Efficient Scrutiny of Government Funding of the Voluntary Sector. Profiting from Partnership (1990), HMSO, London.

Elliott, P. (1972), *The Sociology of the Professions*, MacMillan, London.

Emery, F.E. and Trist, E.L. (1965), *Towards a Social Ecology*, Plenum Publishing, London.

English, J. (1988), *Social Services in Scotland*, Scottish Academic Press, Edinburgh.

Finlayson, G. (1990), "A Moving Frontier", *Twentieth Century British History*, 1 (2), pp. 186-206.

Flexner, A. (1915), "Is social work a profession?", *Proceedings of the 42nd National Conference of Charities and Correction*, Hilman Publishing, Chicago.

171

Forrester, D.B. (1985), *Christianity and the Future of Welfare*, Epworth Press, London.

Forrester, D.B. and Skene, D. (1988), *Just Sharing*, Epworth Press, London.

Foucault, M. (1972), *The Archaeology of Knowledge*, Tavistock, London.

Foucault, M. (1976), *The History of Sexuality, Volume 1*, Random House, New York.

Foucault, M. (1977), *Discipline and Punish*, Allen Lane, London.

Gelsthorpe, L. (1987), "The Differential Treatment of Males and Females in the Criminal Justice System", in Research Highlights in Social Work, *Sex, Gender and Care Work*, Jessica Kingsley, London.

George, M. (1994), "Hey Big Spender", *Community Care*, 23-29 June, pp. 18- 19.

Gilligan, C. (1987), "Woman's Place in Man's Life Cycle", in Harding, S. (ed), *Feminism and Methodology*, Indiana University Press and Open University, Indiana and Milton Keynes, pp. 57-73.

Gladstone, F.J. (1979), *Voluntary Action in a Changing World*, Bedford Square Press, London.

Glaser, B. and Strauss, A. (1967), *The Discovery of Grounded Theory*, Aldine, Chicago.

Gordon, C. (1980), *Foucault, M., Power/Knowledge. Selected Interviews and other Writings 1972-1977*, Harvester Press, Brighton.

Gorham, D. (1978), "The Maiden Tribute of Modern Babylon Re-examined : Child Prostitution and the Idea of Childhood in Late-Victorian England", *Victorian Studies*, Spring.

Greenwood, E. (1957), "Attributes of a Profession", *Social Work*, 2.

Griffiths Report (1988), *Community Care : Agenda for Action*, HMSO, London.

Hadley, R. and Hatch, S. (1981), *Social Welfare and the Failure of the State*, Allen and Unwin, London.

Hale, J. (1984), "Feminism and Social Work Practice", in Jordan B., and Parton, N. (eds), *The Political Dimensions of Social Work*, Basil Blackwell, Oxford.

Hapgood, J. (1983), *Church and Nation in a Secular Age*, Barton, Longman and Todd, London.

Hatch, S. (1980), *Outside the State*, Croom Helm, London.

Hayek, F.A. (1944), *The Road to Serfdom*, Chicago University Press, Chicago.

Henderson, A. (1986), "Christianity and the Psycho-dynamic Approach", in Philpot, T. (ed), *Social Work. A Christian Perspective*, Lion Publishing, Herts.

172

Henriques, F. (1968), *Modern Sexuality. Prostitution and Society, Volume 3*, Panther, London.

Hinton, N. and Clyde, M. (1982), "The Voluntary Sector in the Remodelled Welfare State", *Yearbook of Social Policy, 1980-81*, Routledge and Kegan Paul, London.

Hirst, P. (1981), "The Genesis of the Social", *Politics and Power*, 3.

Hollis, P. (1979), *Women in Public*, Allen and Unwin, London.

Holman, B. (1986), "Working in the Community" in Philpot, T. (ed), *Social Work. A Christian Perspective*, Lion Publishing, Herts., pp. 65-74.

Holman, B. (1988), *Putting Families First*, MacMillan, London.

Hopkinson, A. (1976), *Single Mothers. The First Year*, SCSP, Edinburgh.

Horne, M. (1987), *Values in Social Work*, Wildwood House for Community Care, Hants.

Howe, D. (1986), "The Segregation of Women and their Work in the Personal Social Services", *Critical Social Policy*, 15, Spring.

Hudson, A. (1986), "Troublesome Girls" in *Girls in Trouble - Whose Problem? New approaches to work with young women for social work agencies*, Rainer Foundation, London.

Hudson, A. (1989), "Changing Perspectives : Feminism, Gender and Social Work", in Langan, M. and Lee, P. (eds), *Radical Social Work Today*, Unwin Hyman, London.

Humphries, B. (1976), *Only Connect*, Guild of Service, Edinburgh.

Humphries, E.M. (1983), *The Ideologies of Social Work and Volunteers*, unpublished Ph.D. thesis, University of Edinburgh, Edinburgh.

Illich, I. (1977), *Disabling Professions*, Marion Boyers, London.

James, M. and Jongeward, D. (1971), *Born to Win*, Addison-Wesley Publishing, New York.

Jeffreys, S. (1985), *The Spinster and her Enemies*, Pandora Press, London.

Jeffreys, S. (1987), *The Sexuality Debates*, Routledge and Kegan Paul, London.

Jehu, D. (1972), *Behaviour Modification in Social Work*, John Wiley and Sons, London.

Johnson, N. (1981), *Voluntary Social Services*, Blackwell and Robertson, Oxford.

Johnson, T.J. (1972), *Professions and Power*, MacMillan, London.

Johnson, T.J. (1977), "The Professions in the Class Structure", in Scase, R. (ed), *Industrial Society, Class, Cleavage and Control*, Allen and Unwin, London.

Johnston, J. (1974), "The First Five Years : Success or Failure?", *Focus*, 33, Nov.

173

Johnstone, G. (1988), "The Psychiatric Approach to Crime - A Sociological Analysis", *Economy and Society*, 17 (3) Aug.

Jones, C. (1979), "Social Work Education, 1900-1977", in Parry, N., Rustin M., and Satyamurti, C. (eds), *Social Work, Welfare and the State*, Edward Arnold, London.

Jordan, B. (1984), *Invitation to Social Work*, Martin Robertson, London.

Kadushin, A. (1976), "Men in a Woman's Profession", *Social Work*, 21, pp. 440-447.

Kilbrandon Committee on juvenile delinquents and juveniles in need of care, (1964), HMSO, Edinburgh.

King, J.F.S. (1964), *The Probation Service* (2nd edition), Butterworth, London.

Kirk, H.D. and Kirk, R.V. (1966), *Adoption Services at the Crossroads. The Challenge of Change*, Ontario Association of Children's Aid Societies, Ontario.

Knight, R. (1950), *Intelligence and Intelligence Tests* (5th edition), Methuen, London.

Kramer, R.M. (1981), *Voluntary Agencies in the Welfare State*, University of California Press, California.

Kravetz, D. (1976), "Sexism in a Woman's Profession", *Social Work*, 21, (6), Nov. pp. 421-426.

Kritzman, L.D. (1988), *Michel Foucault. Politics, Philosophy, Culture. Interviews and Other Writings, 1977-1984*, Routledge, New York.

Lamotte, J. (1981), *The Home that Jill Built*, SCSP, Edinburgh.

Land, H. (1991), "Time to Care", in MacLean, M. and Groves, D. (eds), *Women's Issues in Social Policy*, Routledge, London, pp. 7-20.

Langan, M. and Day, L. (1992) *Women, Oppression and Social Work*, Routledge, London.

Langan, M. (1993), "New Directions in Social Work", in Clarke, J. (ed), *A Crisis in Care?*, Open University, Milton Keynes.

Logan, W. (1871), *The Great Social Evil*, Glasgow.

McBoyle Committee on the neglect of children in their own homes (1963), HMSO, Edinburgh.

McBriar, A.M. (1987), *An Edwardian Mixed Doubles*, Clarendon Press, Oxford.

McCaw, P. and McGuire, S. (1980), *Someone Special*, Guild of Service, Edinburgh.

McCaw, P. and Sage, A. (1986), *Further Connections*, Family Care, Edinburgh.

McCrone, D. (1992), *Understanding Scotland*, Routledge, London.

McIntosh, M. (1979), "The Welfare State and the Needs of the Dependent

Family", in Burnam, S. (ed), *Fit Work for Women*, Croom Helm, London.

McWhinnie, A.M. (1966), *Adoption Assessments*, Standing Conference of Societies Registered for Adoption, Edinburgh.

McWhinnie, A.M. (1967), *Adopted Children : How They Grow Up*, Routledge and Kegan Paul, London.

Mahood, L. (1990), *The Magdalenes. Prostitution in the Nineteenth Century*, Routledge, London.

Marsh, D.C. (1970), *The Welfare State*, Longman, London.

Matthews, T. (1989), *What Price Empowerment?*, unpublished M.Sc. Dissertation, University of Edinburgh, Edinburgh.

Matthews, T. (1992), "Poverty, Social Welfare and the Voluntary Sector", in Davidson, R. and Erskine, A. (eds), *Poverty, Deprivation and Social Work*, University of Aberdeen, Aberdeen.

Maxwell, S. (1989), *Riding the Tiger. The Scottish Voluntary Sector in the Market Economy*, SCVO, Edinburgh.

Maynard, M. (1985), "The Response of Social Workers to Domestic Violence", in Pahl, J. (ed), *Private Violence and Public Policy*, Routledge and Kegan Paul, London.

Miller, J. (1859), *Prostitution considered in relation to its Cause and Cure*, Edinburgh.

Miller, J.B. (1983), *Toward a New Psychology of Women*, Penguin, London.

Miller, P. and Rose, N. (1986), *The Power of Psychiatry*, Polity Press, Oxford.

Miller, P. and Rose, N. (1990), "Governing Economic Life", *Economy and Society*, 19 (1) Feb.

Mitchell, J.C. (1983), "Case and Situation Analysis", *Sociological Review*, 31 (2) pp. 187-211.

Mordaunt, J. (1992), *The Funding Game : A Case-study of Voluntary Statutory Relationships*, unpublished Ph.D. thesis, University of Edinburgh, Edinburgh.

Mort, F. (1987), *Dangerous Sexualities*, Routledge and Kegan Paul, London.

Mowat, C.L. (1961), *The Charity Organisation Society, 1869-1913, Its Ideas and its Work*, Methuen, London.

Murray, G.J. (1969), *Voluntary Organisations and Social Welfare*, Oliver and Boyd, Glasgow.

Neill, A.S. (1962), *Summerhill : A Radical Approach to Education*, Gollancz, London.

Nelson, S. (1982), *Incest - Fact and Myth*, Stramullion, Edinburgh.

Newman, N. and Mackintosh, H. (1976), *A Roof over their Heads?*, Edinburgh University, Edinburgh.

Newton, G. (1956), "Trends in Probation Training", *British Journal of Delinquency*, Oct.

Oakley, A. (1981), "Interviewing Women : A Contradiction in Terms", in Roberts, H. (ed), *Doing Feminist Research*, Routledge and Kegan Paul, London.

Parry, N. and Parry, J. (1979), "Social Work, Professionalism, and the State", in Parry N. et al (eds), *Social Work, Welfare and the State*, Edward Arnold, London.

Parsons, T. (1951), *The Social System*, Routledge and Kegan Paul, London.

Parton, N. (1991), *Governing the Family*, MacMillan, London.

Pearson, M. (1972), *The Age of Consent. Victorian Prostitution and its Enemies*, David and Charles Publishers, Newton Abbott.

Pincus, A. and Minahan, A. (1973), *Social Work Practice. Model and Method*, F.E. Peacock, Itasca I.L.

Platt, J. (1981a), "Evidence and Proof in Documentary Research", *Sociological Review*, 29, 1.

Platt, J. (1981b), "On Interviewing One's Peers", *British Journal of Sociology*, 32 (1) pp. 75-91.

Prochaska, F. (1980), *Women and Philanthropy in 19th Century England*, Clarendon Press, Oxford.

Rafter, N.C. (1983), "Chastising the Unchaste", in Cohen, S. and Scull, A. (eds), *Social Control and the State*, Martin Robertson, Oxford, pp. 288-311.

Ramazanoglu, C. (1989), *Feminism and the Contradictions of Oppression*, Routledge, London.

Ramazanoglu, C. (1993), *Up Against Foucault*, Routledge, London.

Rees, S. and Wallace, A. (1982), *Verdicts on Social Work*, Edward Arnold, London.

Riley, D. (1983), *War in the Nursery*, Virago, London.

Riley, D. (1988), *Am I that Name?*, MacMillan, London.

Rogers, C.R. (1951), *Client-Centred Therapy*, Houghton Mifflin, Boston.

Rogers, C.R. (1980), *Way of Being*, Houghton Mifflin, Boston.

Rooff, M. (1957), *Voluntary Societies and Social Policy*, Routledge and Kegan Paul, London.

Rose, N. (1985), *The Psychological Complex*, Routledge and Kegan Paul, London.

Rowbotham, S. (1983), *There's Always been a Women's Movement this Century,* Pandora Press, London.

Rowe, J. (1966), *Parents, Children and Adoption*, Routledge and Kegan Paul, London.

Rowe, J. and Lambert, L. (1973), *Children who Wait*, Association of British Adoption Agencies, London.

Satyamurti, C. (1979), "Care and Control in Local Authority Social Work, in Parry, N., Rustin, M., and Satyamurti, C. (eds), *Social Work, Welfare and the State*, Edward Arnold, London.

Sawicki, J. (1991), *Disciplining Foucault*, Routledge, London.

Seed, P. (1973), *The Expansion of Social Work in Britain*, Routledge and Kegan Paul, London.

Segal, L. and McIntosh, M. (1992), *Sex Exposed. Sexuality and the Pornography Debate*, Virago, London.

Shenkin, A.M. (1967), "The Psychiatric View", in *Report of a Day Conference on Unmarried Mothers and their Medical and Social Needs*, Standing Conference of Societies Registered for Adoption, Edinburgh.

Shrage, L. (1989), "Should Feminists Oppose Prostitution?", *Ethics*, 99 (2), pp. 347-361.

Smart, C. and Smart, B. (1978), *Women, Sexuality and Social Control*, Routledge and Kegan Paul, London.

Smart, C. (1981), "Law and the Control of Women's Sexuality : the case of the 1950s", in Hutter, B. and Williams, G. (eds), *Controlling Women - the Normal and the Deviant*, Croom Helm, London.

Smart, C. (1989), *Feminism and the Power of Law*, Routledge, London.

Smart, C. (1992), *Regulating Womanhood*, Routledge, London.

Smith, F.B. (1976), "Labouchere's Amendment to the Criminal Law Amendment Bill", *Historical Studies*, 17 (67), pp. 165-173.

Smith, D.C. (1987), *Passive Obedience and Prophetic Protest*, Peter Lang, New York.

Social Work and the Community (1966), White Paper, Cmd 3065, HMSO, Edinburgh.

Specht, H. and Vickery, A. (1977), *Integrating Social Work Methods*, Allen and Unwin, London.

Stanley, L. and Wise, S. (1983), *Breaking Out. Feminist Consciousness and Feminist Research*, Routledge and Kegan Paul, London.

Stanley, L. (1990), *Feminist Praxis*, Routledge, London.

Stone, M. (1984), *All Change in Child Care*, unpublished paper, Queen's College, Glasgow, September.

Stone, M. (1985), "The Boot is on the Other Foot", *Community Care*, August 29, pp. 21-23.

Storkey, E. (1985), *What's Right with Feminism?*, SPCK, London.

Sutherland, J.D. (1989), *Fairbairn's Journey into the Interior*, Free Association Books, London.

Taylor, B. (1983), *Eve and the New Jerusalem*, Virago, London.

Thane, P. (1982), *The Foundations of the Welfare State*, Longman, London.

Thompson, P. (1981) "Life Histories and the Analysis of Social Change", in Bertaux, D. (ed), *Biography and Society*, Sage, Beverly Hills.

Thomson, G.H. (1939), *The Factorial Analysis of Human Ability*, University of London Press, London.

Timms, N. (1962), *Casework in the Childcare Service*, Butterworth, London.

Timms, N. (1970), *Social Work. An Outline for the Intending Student*, Routledge and Kegan Paul, London.

Toren, N. (1972), *Social Work : the case of a semi-profession*, Sage, New York.

Towle, C. (1969), in Perlman, H.H. (ed), *Helping*, University of Chicago Press, Chicago.

Vernon, P.E. (1979), *Intelligence Testing, 1928-1978 What Next?* Scottish Council for Research in Education, Edinburgh.

Volunteer Centre (1975), *Training for Voluntary Service. Co-ordinators in the Health and Social Services*, Volunteer Centre.

Walkowitz, J.R. and D.J. (1974), "We are not Beasts of the Field. Prostitution and the Poor in Plymouth and Southampton under the Contagious Diseases Acts", in Hartman, M. and Banner, L.W. (eds), *Clio's Consciousness Raised*, Harper and Row, New York.

Walkowitz, J. (1980), *Prostitution and Victorian Society - Women, Class and the State*, Cambridge University Press, Cambridge.

Walkowitz, J. (1982), "Male Vice and Feminist Virtue. Feminism and the Politics of Prostitution in Nineteenth Century Britain", *History Workshop*, 13, pp. 79-93.

Walton, R.G. (1975), *Women in Social Work*, Routledge and Kegan Paul, London.

Ware, H.R.E. (1969), *The Recruitment, Regulation and Role of Prostitution in Britain from the middle of the Nineteenth Century to the Present Day*, unpublished Ph.D. thesis, University of London, London.

Warnock, M. (1984), *Report of the Committee of Inquiry into Human Fertilisation and Embryology*, HMSO, Cmnd 9314, London.

Watney, S. (1987), *Policing Desire*, Methuen, London.

Webb, A. and Wistow, G. (1987), *Social Work, Social Care and Social Planning*, Longman, London.

Weeks, J. (1981), *Sex, Politics and Society*, Longman, London.

Weeks, J. (1985), *Sexuality and its Discontents*, Routledge and Kegan Paul, London.

Wilenski, H.L. (1964), "The Professionalization of Everyone?", *American Journal of Sociology*, LXX (2) Sept. pp. 142-146.

Wilson, B.R. (1966), *Religion in a Secular Society*, Watts, London.

178

Wilson, E. (1977), *Women and the Welfare State*, Tavistock, London.

Wilson, E. (1983), "Feminism and Social Policy", in Loney M. et al (eds), *Social Policy and Social Welfare*, Open University Press, Milton Keynes.

Winnicott, D.W. and Britton, C. (1944), "The Problem of Homeless Children", in *Children's Communities*, New Education Monograph, 1.

Winnicott, D.W. (1957), *The Child, the Family and the Outside World*, Tavistock, London.

Wise, S. (1990), "Becoming a Feminist Social Worker", in Stanley, L. (ed), *Feminist Praxis*, Routledge, London.

Witz, A. (1990), "Patriarchy and Professions : The Gendered Politics of Occupational Closure", *Sociology* 24 (4) Nov. pp. 675-690.

Wolfenden Committee (1978), *The Future of Voluntary Organisations*, Croom Helm, London.

Woodroofe, K. (1962), *From Charity to Social Work*, Routledge and Kegan Paul, London.

Wootten, B. (1959), *Social Science and Social Pathology*, Allen and Unwin, London.

Wright, F.D. (1986), *Left to Care Alone*, Gower, Aldershot.

Yelloly, M.A. (1975), *Professional Ideologies in British Social Work*, unpublished Ph.D. thesis, University of Leicester, Leicester.

Yelloly, M.A. (1980), *Social Work Theory and Psychoanalysis*, Van Nostrand Reinhold, New York.

Young, L. (1954), *Out of Wedlock*, McGraw Hill, New York.

Younghusband, E. (1947), *Report on the Employment and Training of Social Workers*, Carnegie UK Trust, London.

Younghusband, E. (1964), *Social Work and Social Change*, Allen and Unwin, London.

Younghusband, E. (1978), *Social Work in Britain, 1950 - 1975*, Allen and Unwin, London.

Younghusband, E. (1981), *The Newest Profession. A Short History of Social Work*, IPC, Community Care, London.